Praise for *A Hole in the Ocean: A Hamptons' Apprenticeship*

"These irresistibly amusing and engaging recollections of the author's encounters with the great and near-great artists and poets who washed ashore in the Hamptons has a special charm, as our intrepid protagonist plays unofficial chauffeur, therapist, straight-man and witness, always with retrospective self-awareness, insight and bittersweet gratitude."

—PHILLIP LOPATE

"Sandy McIntosh writes like a combination of Dostoevsky and Woody Allen."

—MARY MACKEY

"Deliciously droll. Stars-in-the-eyes young poet meets literary and art world icons in the Hamptons. And re-meets and reconsiders. And admires. And continues to honor and to create his own work."

—LAURA WELLS, *The East Hampton Star*

"Intelligence, foresight and wit.... There is something here that is at once deep, engaging and profound."

—NEIL LEADBEATER, *Galatea Resurrects*

"*A Hole in the Ocean* is a beautiful written recollection of a simpler time on the east end when main streets were quiet even during the summer and one could hear `the crashing of the ocean waves a half-mile away.' e.e. cummings said `A hole in the ocean will never be missed.' Neither should this book."

—BRIAN CUDZILO, *Dan's Papers*

Also by Sandy McIntosh

Poetry Collections

Earth Works

Which Way to the Egress?

Monsters of the Antipodes

Endless Staircase

Between Earth and Sky

Selected Poems of H.R. Hays (editor)

The After-Death History of My Mother

Forty-Nine Guaranteed Ways to Escape Death

237 More Reasons to Have Sex (collaboration with Denise Duhamel)

Ernesta, In the Style of the Flamenco

Cemetery Chess: Collected and New Poems

Prose

A Hole In the Ocean: A Hamptons Apprenticeship

The Poets in the Poets-In-the-Schools

From a Chinese Kitchen

Firing Back (collaboration with Jodi-Beth Galos)

Computer Software

The Best of Wok Talk

Mavis Beacon Teaches Typing!

Lost in Literature

Lesser Lights

More Tales from a Hamptons' Apprenticeship

Sandy McIntosh

A VOLUME IN THE CHAPTER ONE SERIES

MARSH HAWK PRESS
East Rockaway, New York • 2019

Marsh Hawk books are published by Marsh Hawk Press, Inc., a not-for-profit corporation under section 501(c)3 United States Internal Revenue Code.

Book design: Susan Quasha

Library of Congress Cataloging-in-Publication Data
Names: McIntosh, Sandy, 1947- author.
Title: Lesser lights : more tales from a Hamptons' apprenticeship / Sandy McIntosh.
Other titles: More tales from a Hamptons' apprenticeship
Description: New York : Marsh Hawk Press, [2019]
Identifiers: LCCN 2018023766 | ISBN 9780996991131 (pbk)
Subjects: LCSH: McIntosh, Sandy, 1947—Friends and associates. | Poets, American—20th century—Biography. | Art and literature—New York (State).
 | Hamptons (N.Y.)—Social life and customs.
Classification: LCC PS3613.C54 Z46 2018 | DDC 811/.6 [B] —dc23 LC record available at https://lccn.loc.gov/2018023766

Marsh Hawk Press
P.O. Box 206
East Rockaway, New York 11518-0206
www.marshhawkpress.org

Personal Thanks

For my generous and inspiring editor, Mary Mackey. For my colleagues and friends, Thomas Fink and George Whitson. For Francis Smith, who, in many pre-dawn sessions, cheered on Robert's evolving scandals. Thanks to Jackie and Mel Moss, Gretchen Berger, and Graham Everett for filling in the missing pieces.

And always for my wife, Barbara.

CONTENTS

Epilogue

Introduction
The Night Jackson Pollack Died

"We'd been having a musical evening at Alfonso Ossorio's studio the night Jackson Pollack died," H. R. Hays said. "The sky was like to-night: clear, balmy. I think someone was playing a jazz sax. Dreamy. I drifted off. Then my wife Julie was shaking me. 'Wake up Hoffman,' she whispered. 'Look over there.' I looked and saw those police emergency lights down at the end of the road."

"Are you sure?" asked David Ignatow. "I thought Pollock was killed on Springs Fireplace Road—that hairpin curve."

"Well," said Hays petulantly. "That's where we all were at the time. On Springs Fireplace Road. That's where Alfonso Ossorio lived. Right after that hairpin curve."

"That was in the '50s. I didn't even live here then," said Ignatow.

"We weren't talking about you. Not everything has to be about you," muttered Hays.

As a twenty year-old student and poet, I was happy to be sitting with them that night, listening to their stories and their bickering on the Hays' second floor porch at his home in the East Hampton woods. Happy that they were interested in me and in the things I was struggling to write. In fact, I couldn't believe my luck.

In 1966, after six distressing years in military school, I had enrolled at Southampton College. It was then a branch of Long Island University, since dissolved. Its mission was to serve local students, the children of farmers and shopkeepers who served the wealthy summer residents living near the Atlantic Ocean. Most students attending the college had practical career objectives. Few had any interest in the humanities, especially in painting, creative writing, sculpture or serious music. The college, having failed to lure established academics from metropolitan universities to what was for nine months of the year a desolate rural environment, had to resort to hiring locals with uncertain academic certifications to teach those students who might be interested in the arts. But the Hamptons being the Hamptons, the local artists and writers included in the faculty at that time came immediately to resemble the quietly shimmering artist-teachers of the innovative, short-lived, experimental Black Mountain College in Asheville, North Carolina, at which some of them had actually taught. For instance, at Southampton Willem de Kooning lectured on painting; Ilya Bolotowsky, the neo-plasticist painter with a thick Russian accent, taught Freshman English. Among poets teaching were the Bollingen Prize winner David Ignatow, and the pioneering performance poet Charles Matz. The playwright and poet H. R. Hays headed the Theater Department.

Why did a group of distinguished artists and writers congregate at a new, undistinguished college? "You see," de Kooning told me after we'd become acquainted. "In the wintertime, they're here all alone. They work in their studios all day and then want to get together at night, usually at Bobby Van's, or some other bar. Then they get into a fight—Jim Jones likes to throw punches—or get drunk and the police take them to jail. It's either that or they meet at the college and have a good time without getting into too much trouble." "The truth is," Ilya Bolotowsky added. "We're all exiles."

I came to believe that Bolotowsky was right. Hays, Ignatow, Bolotowsky and de Kooning were not only exiles, they recognized me as one, too, and to my delight became my mentors and friends during my college days and for many years after.

I

Taking Reality Through Its Paces
Filmmaking with Ilya Bolotowsky and Norman Mailer

ON THE ROAD between Noyac and Sag Harbor, there once stood an inn called the Hilltop House, run by an allegedly sadomasochistic dentist from New York City. Each weekend the inn's rooms, restaurant and swimming pool attracted crowds of exotic guests, some of them notorious, like the strung-out musicians of Andy Warhol's band, the *Velvet Underground*, and others not so notorious, but possibly just as strung-out. By the middle of the summer my friend Dick had taken a job as a waiter in the restaurant. He'd been hired earlier to paint a mural on the side of an ugly building on Montauk Highway in Watermill, but the owner had refused to compensate him for the gallons of paint he'd bought on credit. The project was abandoned with only half the mural done, so Dick had taken the waiter's job in order to pay off his creditors.

The Hilltop's restaurant was always crowded and noisy, and the air bushy with cigarette and marijuana smoke. This didn't bother Dick, as he made his way among the tables, often mixing up the orders, but serving them to ravenous customers who were grateful to be given anything to eat. "The only thing that drives me nuts," Dick told me, "is the noise when I'm trying to sleep." According to Dick, his room adjoined the owner's suite, and his late nights and early mornings were tortured by the screams apparently coming from the young men—putative "sons"—that the dentist owner brought to the inn each weekend.

Adding to the usual crowd and chaos one weekend, Norman Mailer arrived with about one hundred people whom he intended to use in making his film, *Maidstone*. A few of Mailer's crew were professional actors, such as Rip Torn and Ultra Violet from Andy Warhol's films, and technical people, such as the filmmakers D. A. Pennebacker and Buddy Wirtschafter (recruited as an actor). However, most were amateurs—friends of Mailer or friends of friends who happened to be in the area and wanted to get in on the avant-garde action. Three of the latter were fixtures of East Hampton: the artist Alfonso Ossorio; the founder of Grove Press, Barney Rosset; and the owner of Gardiner's Island, Robert David Lion Gardiner. Mailer filmed key scenes at their homes.

Mailer also planned to make his film in three days. In accordance with his theory of "pure" cinema, he had not written a script and had only outlined the central characters, intending that the pressure of the three-day round-the-clock shooting schedule would force his professionals and amateurs to improvise something real and dangerous. Danger seemed likely, since, besides the drugs and alcohol that already pervaded the place, rumors persisted that some of Mailer's people were carrying firearms. More than once, Rip Torn, said to be frustrated by the unprofessional antics of his fellow actors, was observed eyeing the carpenter's hammer that he would eventually use to assault Mailer on the final day of filming.

Meanwhile, in another part of the forest (and this is not a fanciful way of putting it, since at the time there was much "unimproved" woodland in the area), Ilya Bolotowsky was assembling a crew to make a film on a more modest scale, yet with similar unscripted "pure" film intent.

Bolotowsky had been born in St. Petersburg in either 1897 or 1907 (depending upon which version of his autobiographical sketches you read). Already an artist when he immigrated to New York City, he continued to study while taking work as a textile designer. In 1933, he discovered Piet Mondrian's two dimensional grid pattern paintings, as well as the more figurative and lyric paintings of Miró. He incorporated both into his own work, which now included playful biomorphic forms and rectangular planes of unmodulated color. Within a few years, however, he had dispensed with the playful forms and given his work over to the strictness of the Mondrian-inspired discipline Neo-plasticism. He had enjoyed success with his work during the 1950s, and had been asked to lecture at various institutions, including the famous experimental college, Black Mountain, where poets, such as Ignatow, Charles Olson, and Robert Creeley, and painters, such as de Kooning also taught.

Given his long career as a painter, it was odd, then, for me to meet Bolotowsky in his guise as my Freshman English professor. He was a short, jovial man with a pronounced Russian accent, nearly bald head and thick, white, drooping walrus moustache, which, he informed us, measured sixteen inches on each side. That semester Bolotowsky led us through the mysteries of James Joyce, beginning with *Portrait of the Artist as a Young Man*, and coming back full circle to an earlier version of the same work, *Stephen Hero*. Perhaps I suspect that only a few of us reveled in these sophisticated works. He led our discussions as a practicing artist, not a literary critic. That is to say, Bolotowsky's interest lay in showing us useful techniques in the service of achieving some effect without reference to any tradition writers and other artists might be extending or establishing along the way. This seemed quite logical to me since traditions and the literary or artistic theories that describe them were only secondary concerns of painters, writers, sculptors whom I met in the Hamptons, and, as Bolotowsky said, theories needn't concern us in his classroom. Again and again, he showed us how Joyce and other writers achieved their narrative effects by referring to the work of contemporaneous visual artists

When I asked him to describe what went on in his own painting, he told me the Neo-plastic style was "the most meaningful and exciting direction in art. As a Neo-plasticist, I strive after an ideal of harmony," he said, stroking the left side of his moustache. "Neo-plasticism can achieve unequaled tension, equilibrium, and harmony through the relation of the vertical and horizontal elements."

That was it: no over-arching concerns, no looking back over his shoulder to his place in history, only a concentration on the work at hand. "This is the way you might want to approach your own writing," he suggested.

(Bolotowsky was pleased when, as editor of the college newspaper and the underground magazine, *Survivors' Manual*, I published a few of his one-act plays. In return, when the college published a book of my poetry, Bolotowsky painted the cover illustration.)

Bolotowsky often invited me to his small studio in Sag Harbor to see his new work: round canvasses—tondos—and rectangular columns of various heights on which he was able to extend his two-dimensional paintings to the column's four contiguous sides. One element of his work—or rather, the lack of it—disturbed me, though. The "tension, equilibrium, and harmony through the relation of the vertical and horizontal elements" I could understand. But why were his works so dry, so unemotional?

"My paintings are pure abstractions that remain austere, but always the same to the viewer, no matter how he or she is feeling at the time," he said. "Emotions, on the other hand are temporary. I save my emotions for my films."

Bolotowsky had organized film festivals at the college at which he had shown some of his own movies, as well as those of the early experiments of artistic film, such as Hans Richter's *Ballet Mechaneque*, and the notorious Dali-Buñuel surrealist shocker, *Un Chien Andalou*. I was impressed with Bolotowsky's films less because of their narrative subject matter (he used or perhaps invented myths—and set them in modern dress), and more because they featured the naked breasts of various co-eds I'd lusted after. When, in the summer when Mailer was making *Maidstone*, Bolotowsky asked me to be in one of his films, I was happy to accept, and even suggested that I would bring some friends with me who might also be in his movie.

Bolotowsky agreed, and the night before filming was to begin, I invited my friends to the Hilltop House for drinks so that we could make arrangements.

By 11:00 o'clock that night, the parking lot and lawns of Hilltop House were filled with cars. Dick and his friend Wendy, a tall, beautiful Shinnecock Indian, met us. "You're never going to get anything to eat tonight," he told me. "That guy" he said, and pointed to a short man with frizzy hair who was haranguing a crowd of staggering, giggling people wandering about inside the windowed building that served as an indoor dining room and dance floor. "That guy ordered all the food we had in house, and they ate up everything. We've been turning people away." We could get drinks, Dick said, although, we might not find a place to sit. We headed for the bar.

As soon as I walked into the drunken melee, I recognized the short, frizzy-haired man who had ordered up all the food as Norman Mailer.

The only seats available, it turned out, were at the entrance to the room in which Mailer and his crew were meeting. We sat, and I, at least, became absorbed in what Mailer was saying—yelling, actually.

"We hope to prove," Mailer was arguing, "that one can make a beautiful, tasteful, resonant, touching, evocative picture by using cinema *vérité* methods in four days. If we can do it, a lot of people out in Hollywood are going to commit suicide. Well," he went on, "it's something to work for. Help stamp out mediocrity."

"Right now, the film does not exist as a plot, only a presence. But it's going to be a film about beauty, intrigue, and the subtle nature of reality—how difficult it is to know what reality is until you take it through its paces. It's going to be a film about a notorious movie director who has come to the east end of Long Island ostensibly to look at sites for his new film. Now, this film within a film is going to be a sexual spoof of *Belle de Jour*, this time with a male house of assignation to which women come. In the house will be a bunch of male stars, the director's rat pack, which we're going to call the Cash Box. By the way," he added with a wry smile. "I'm playing the part of Norman T. Kingsley, the lead."

Mailer's crew had mostly settled down to listen to him, although he had had to shout for order several times. It seemed that only my friends were restless, getting up from the table to get drinks or chatting noisily to one another. At one point Mailer looked directly at us. "You're either in the film or you're not," he thundered.

"We're not in your film," one of my friends shouted back.

"Then get the hell out of here, all of you in the back!"

As most of Mailer's crew turned to watch, my friends and I got up to leave. When Wendy stood, however, Mailer thrust up his hand like a traffic cop. "Not you," he ordered. "I want you in the film." Thus, Wendy abandoned us to join Mailer.

The following morning, I was able to corral my three friends to meet with Bolotowsky. I had been renting a cottage at the end of Springs Fireplace Road, across from Gardiner's Island. My friends included next-door neighbors John (a sculptor) and his wife, Helen (a high school teacher), and my girlfriend, Elizabeth. John specialized in sculpting huge marble penises, although his favorite was one he'd carved from ivory. "I polish it every day," he said, "It gets a wonderful luster." John was eager to be in the film, especially after I told him about Bolotowsky's penchant for nudity.

"I don't think he's particularly interested in *male* nudity," I'd warned John, but he decided to give it a shot, anyway.

Elizabeth was upset with me about something horrible I had allegedly done or said to her, which I had been too drunk to remember, and after returning from the Hilltop House, she'd taken her suitcase and moved out of my cottage and into the extra room in John's. Apparently, she spent the next hour or so complaining about my crime to John's wife, who was sympathetic and consoling. The next morning, neither Helen nor Elizabeth was speaking me.

We met up with Bolotowsky, his son, Andrew, Andrew's girlfriend, Jane, and another Helen (a college student whom I'd remembered from Bolotowsky's previous films) at Peter Wrangell's home in Noyac. Bolotowsky confided to me that Peter was a direct descendant of the famous Wrangell family in Russia. In fact, he told me with some awe, Peter was nobility.

Bolotowsky appeared with his sixteen-millimeter camera and we gathered around for a smaller, more modest version of a Mailer-type briefing. Bolotowsky had no great directorial philosophy to share. A patch of woodland surrounded Wrangell's house, and he told us we would be using the woods and some dilapidated buildings for the film. There was also a small, swampy lake nearby, and we might use that location, too.

"What would you like us to do?" I asked.

"Well," he answered looking around. "Why don't we go over to that old barn and see what happens." Like Mailer, Bolotowsky had no script, and would be content to film while reality took us through its paces.

That afternoon, while Bolotowsky was trying to figure out whether to push us all into the lake, Mailer began filming at Barney Rosset's house. Five camera crews wandered over the property, filming the actors who either did or did not improvise scenes on cue, but seemed to prefer drinking from Rosset's unlimited supply of alcohol. The house was enormous, with two swimming pools (indoor and outdoor), abundant lawns and trees, and a wandering garden. One of many journalists following the adventure reported that it reminded her of a surrealistic Buckingham Palace garden party.

Mailer arrived and busied himself with greeting actors and crew, and partying with friends and his ex-wives, who had shown up. At a point dictated by some personal sense of propriety, he got down to business and demanded a cast list.

An assistant appeared and promised to make one up in an hour.

"An hour? An hour? Make it fifteen minutes. Where's a camera? I need a camera," Mailer continued, turning to someone else. "You! Are you the last functional camera left in America?"

As Mailer's shape-shift from party guest to demon movie director was noticed, the crowd gradually put down their drinks and gathered around, awaiting orders. He split them into five crews, each assigned a camera operator and different location on the property, and filming-proper began.

Back at Peter Wrangell's, Bolotowsky took me aside. "Why don't you organize something for the first scene?" he said, looking around distractedly, as if hunting for something he'd dropped in the grass.

Surprised and flattered that he would be interested in my ideas, I suggested that we punch holes in the plaster walls and stick our heads through them. (I had really loved the old surrealist films he'd shown our class.) Bolotowsky conferred with Wrangell, and Wrangell trotted back to his house from which he returned with an assortment of hats—straw boaters and ladies' flowered sun hats, a top hat and a bowler. He also produced a handful of cigars and handed them out. I took the bowler hat, lit my cigar and positioned myself behind the hole I'd punched in the wall. Hats on and cigars lit, everyone else did the same until the view from the camera showed a gallery of disembodied heads with hats, clouds of cigar smoke coming from our mouths. Bolotowsky directed us to talk to each other animatedly, and we did. Since the film wasn't to have sound, it didn't matter so much what we talked about as that we did it with enthusiasm.

That scene completed, we moved on. Someone suggested something we could do, and Bolotowsky agreed to do it. We did that, then followed the suggestions of others in the group, until we'd filmed eight or ten unrelated scenes.

"What's this movie going to be about?" I whispered to Bolotowsky. I'd been happy to perform in the scenes, but the process reminded me of the extemporaneous eight-millimeter home movies I'd made as a twelve year-old. My friends and I had concentrated our cinematography then on endless variations of the theme: Kid (or Kid-like dummy) falls off roof; falls out of tree; is thrown through window; etc., and lands on the ground with a bloody splat. This film seemed to me to be at approximately that same, unexalted level, at that point.

Bolotowsky, essentially a subtle, quiet man with twinkling eyes and a soft, insinuating chuckle, was reticent about what he was doing until someone pressed him. "You'll see," was all he answered.

Heedless, I pressed on. "But don't you have some theme in mind that we could work on together? It might help us focus on what you want."

After a moment during which he looked at me silently, he replied. "The theme is emerging now, as we do each scene. When we finish, we'll know what we have. But it's all in the editing. Why don't you exercise some patience?"

Chastened, I promised I would.

John, the sculptor, then came forward with his suggestion. He'd gone through the previous scenes, but I had noticed his growing impatience. "Why don't we take that rowboat over there and go out on the lake?"

"Hmm," hummed Bolotowsky and rubbed his chin, considering the idea. "Very well," he answered. "Why don't we have all the girls take off their clothes and go out in that boat on the lake?"

Now we were getting somewhere, the voyeur in me silently cheered. We dragged the little boat by its rope to the lake. The girls began to undress, and I was enjoying the scene, when John began taking off his clothes, too. "Come on," he shouted, now full of bright enthusiasm. "Let's all take off our clothes!"

Wrangell smiled and Bolotowsky surreptitiously giggled, but both held up their hands, demurring. I'd been standing next to them, holding some props, and I wondered if I should join the nudists. Bolotowsky looked over at me, obviously reading my mind. "Stay here with me. I'd like you to take notes for continuity."

Somewhat relieved, I took the notebook in which one of the women had been recording the order of scenes we'd filmed, and picked up where she'd left off.

Bolotowsky's camera was rolling. John had the girls get into the boat, and he pushed off into the water, pulling himself aboard. The little boat drifted several feet toward the center of the lake, rocking each time John leapt up to display himself to the girls and to the camera. When he did this, I heard Bolotowsky's tongue click, and he'd utter some mumble of displeasure.

After that, Jane and Helen (the college student) modestly dressed themselves, but John, his wife and my girlfriend, Elizabeth, insisted on doing their scenes in the nude. John soon made himself annoying by leaping in front of the camera holding his penis and shaking it. By the evening, when we quit, only Elizabeth seemed fascinated—or, to be frank, mesmerized—by John the Satyr's antics.

After we finished filming, I drove everyone back to the Fireplace Road cottages. Neither Elizabeth nor Helen said a word to me. Only John wanted to talk, and then only to brag about his uninhibited frolicking in front of the camera. When I asked them what we should do for dinner, Helen answered. "We're not going out for dinner tonight," she told me, with a chilly smile. "We're staying in. That is, we're staying in bed. All of us except you. You are not invited." I couldn't help noticing that Helen was holding Elizabeth's hand and that Elizabeth was refusing to look at me. No matter how many times I begged her to tell me what I had said or done that was so bad, she only turned away.

Feeling low, I dropped them off, then turned my car around and headed over to the Hilltop House to see what was going on there.

Around that time, as the sun began to set and the natural light fade, Mailer's crew wrapped up its shooting for the day. According to one journalist who had been watching the filming, Barney Rosset's garden looked like a set for *La Dolce Vita*, with bottles and people scattered all over the grass, the sound assistants being quietly sick in the bushes, and naked actors refusing to come out of the swimming pool. But gradually, everyone followed Mailer's exit and returned for an early dinner.

Surprisingly, the Hilltop House's parking lot was relatively uncrowded. My friend Dick met me at the door and, as he didn't seem to be busy, I told him all about the day's shooting with Bolotowsky, even describing what was happening right then, in the cottage on Fireplace Road. When Dick asked with a leer why I wasn't there with them, I waved his question away. "Really not my scene." It was too early in the evening and I wasn't yet drunk enough to begin questioning myself about why I was here and not there.

I had dinner, walked around aimlessly, finally arriving at the large room where I'd first seen Mailer and his crew. The place was deserted except for a pianist playing a Chopin waltz—not with great skill, but with real feeling. Sitting down, I was able to get a good look at the pianist: a little man, a dwarf. Why, after my day of bizarre, surrealistic happenings, his appearance should startle me, I can't say. Not noticing me, he continued to play Chopin's sad, delicate music.

When he was done I cleared my throat and told him that his playing was beautiful.

"Thank you," he replied in a child's voice with an accent I took to be French. "I am Hervé. I am an actor in the film being made here. Are you also an actor in the film?"

I told him I wasn't, but that, in fact, I was an actor in another film being made elsewhere.

He stood up from the piano bench—or, in truth, dropped from the bench to the floor—walked over and shook my hand.

"You see my clothes?" he asked. Surreptitiously, I had been glancing at his wet, discolored, wrinkled clothes. "I fell in a swimming pool," he explained. "Everyone thought I was drowning, but I wasn't drowning."

He stopped and looked at me.

"Why did you fall into the swimming pool?" I asked dutifully.

"I fell into the swimming pool because I was drunk," he answered, smiling triumphantly. "I thought I would make a beautiful swan dive, but maybe I just fell in. I knew there were others around watching me fall, but nobody did anything to help. I floated on my face for a while. I studied the bottom of the pool. There were many beer bottles down there. It was like a dream. I almost fell asleep. But at the last second I pulled myself out. Nobody offered me a towel, but some nice man gave me another drink."

From his speech I surmised that he was still drunk.

"I go to bed now," he said, and began to wander through the tangle of chairs, supporting himself on one and then another as he passed, more gracefully than I'd imagined he was capable.

The room was now empty except for me, and I, too, decided that it was time to go. I drove myself home. From my bedroom window I could see that the lights in John's bedroom were still on.

To almost all observers, the next day on Mailer's film set was chaos, with actors blundering through each other's improvised scenes, loudly arguing near the live sound equipment and even fighting. Mailer himself got into a punching match with an actor who had been bothering him with suggestions since the beginning of shooting. On the other hand, Ultra Violet, a star of Andy Warhol's films, was impressed with everyone's energy. "It's all so organized," she said. "Andy's films are never like this."

In the afternoon, the rumor spread that nude scenes were about to be shot; no one was sure where, though. Finally, somebody pointed to the pool house, where several women and D. A. Pennebaker carrying his camera, had just appeared. People watched expectantly for the disrobing, but Pennebaker ushered his group inside, closed and locked the door. Oddly, for such an uninhibited project, all the nude scenes where shot in private.

Mailer divided his crew into units and ordered them to several locations for the afternoon's work. One group ended up at David Lion Gardiner's house on Main Street in East Hampton, the other at Ossorio's mansion. Ossorio's was crammed with paintings, including over one hundred Dubuffets. Many of these were hung on the backs of doors, since the walls were too crowded to accept them. Thus, drunken actors using the bathrooms or bedrooms at various times blindly collided with the valuable artworks as they staggered around, causing some expensive damage.

Bolotowsky filmed the last scenes of his movie in the yard next to my cottage on Fireplace Road. He had heard about the post-filming orgy of the previous night and seemed worried. "The less said about that, the better," he muttered to me.

Nevertheless, he picked up on the hostility that had been growing between John and me, and decided to film us fighting to the death. Someone (possibly the resourceful Peter Wrangell) produced dueling swords. It happened that I had a red shirt with puffy sleeves that always made me feel like a pirate when I wore it. Bolotowsky was delighted with my shirt. John and I faced each other and began clanging and cracking our blades together and dancing about like Errol Flynn, our left arms raised behind us. Unlike the action on Mailer's set, however, neither of us drew blood.

Other scenes were improvised. I had to pick up my sword for a second time to battle a long rubber snake that was lunging and otherwise menacing me, manipulated by somebody off-screen.

After a few hours, Bolotowsky announced that he'd run out of film, and therefore our work on the movie was done. Reflecting on what we'd accomplished over the past two days, I still couldn't see how Bolotowsky might forge coherence from our cinematic commotion. Certainly, the girls' nudity would be interesting in itself, and John's prancing about, penis in hand, would have shock value, but other than those things, I hadn't a clue. However, Bolotowsky had told me that the narrative would emerge by itself from the action, and I trusted that he knew what he was doing.

The next afternoon, while Mailer and crew were wrapping up their shooting on Gardiner's Island, I was at home at my typewriter. I'd been noodling around on the keys, hoping for a poem to take shape, when I had an idea. Why not write a story about Bolotowsky's movie, including everything that had happened in front of and also behind the cameras? I had been looking for something to publish that would get a wider circulation than my poetry, which was printed in little magazines, and it seemed to me that this would be a perfect story for the *Village Voice*.

I decided to call Bolotowsky to tell him my idea. He had often told me of his own publicity schemes, which included flying a stunt airplane in dangerous, seemingly suicidal maneuvers ("I did that to drive up the price of my paintings," he confided). Surely, a story in the *Village Voice* would enhance his reputation as an au courante, cutting-edge artist.

I got him on the phone, but he didn't seem particularly thrilled by my idea. He said, "Hmm. Hmm," a few times, then abruptly told me goodbye.

An hour later, his son Andrew called. They—Bolotowsky and his whole family—would like to discuss my idea with me. Could they come over to my cottage right away? A bit confused and intimidated by Andrew's seriousness, I told them to come over; I'd wait for them.

They arrived in Bolotowsky's old station wagon. Bolotowsky, his wife, Meta (who I'd first seen in an early Bolotowsky film with the appropriate title, *Metanoia*), Andrew, Jane and Helen, the college student, walked single file into my living room and sat down on my old couch. Their faces were solemn, and only Bolotowsky spoke to me.

"I don't think you should write a newspaper story about the filming. This is a private affair, and I wouldn't want word to get out about the other things that happened. Such a story would harm my reputation as a painter, and I won't have that."

His fierce tone was intimidating. I wasn't sure how to answer him. Whether or not I wrote a story was my business. I certainly didn't intend to hurt him, but the reality of what happened was unalterable. Why shouldn't I report it? Was he worried that I'd suggest that he or his family members had been involved in the sexual shenanigans that followed the first day of shooting?

I tried to reassure him of my good intentions, but he didn't seem satisfied. The best I could do was to tell him that I'd think about his request. As silently as they'd entered my house, Bolotowsky and family filed out.

A week passed during which I tried to speak with Bolotowsky, but he wasn't taking my calls. I had made the decision not to write the story and I'd wanted him to know it. One afternoon, I dropped in unannounced at his painting studio. He was cold to me, but showed me some of the paintings he was completing. I told him of my decision, and he accepted it without saying much. Believing that I was not wanted there, I left. I didn't hear from him for several more weeks.

Meanwhile, on Gardiner's Island, while Mailer was lecturing his crew on the alleged philosophical underpinnings of what they'd been filming during the previous days; Rip Torn emerged from a nearby tool shed with a hammer. The cameras were still rolling, and Torn, an insane glint in his eyes, still in character, shouted at Mailer, "Norman

T. Kingsley, I have something for you." He then smashed Mailer on the head three times, drawing blood, before Mailer wrestled him to the ground, clenching Torn's ear between his teeth and biting it open. Later, Torn declared that he had simply been acting, that he hadn't intended to cause Mailer pain. Mailer, however, wasn't buying it, and refused to speak to Torn.

Several weeks after that, as an unexpected conclusion to one of its bacchanalian evenings, the Hilltop House caught fire and burnt to the ground. By then Mailer and his crew—as well as Bolotowky's—were long gone.

Mailer was in New York editing his film, a job that would take him and his assistants four months to complete. It was a question of finding the innate reality of the film, he'd reported, and then, by careful editing, exposing it, making its meaning plain. As the film took shape, Mailer found that his attitude towards his attacker, Rip Torn, was undergoing a change.

Writing of himself in the third person, Mailer later explained his change of heart this way: "So, at this point next day in the filming of *Maidstone*, on the lazy afternoon... the director had come to the erroneous conclusion his movie was done, even though the film was still continuing in the collective mind of some working photographers before whom—as we know all to well—the director was yet to get hit on the head by a hammer wielded by his best actor... a fight [that would] give him a whole new conception of his movie." Torn's attack, Mailer now realized, was not some personal and irrelevant vendetta. Indeed, Torn's action and Mailer's reaction, Mailer saw, were absolutely essential to the movie's reality. Without them, his film would never have achieved the perfection of pure film he now confidently asserted. Because of his realization, Mailer cordially invited Rip Torn to the film's premiere.

After many weeks of silence, Bolotowsky called. He invited me to a screening of our newly edited film. He seemed pleased with the result. At his home, I met Andrew, Meta, Jane and Helen.

It was unique and exciting for me (in this time before video camcorders) to watch myself in action. And the film as a whole pleased me. Bolotowsky had managed to splice together scenes that seemed to have some relationship to each other in terms of cause and effect, and a theme that I sensed but couldn't articulate was emerging. When we got to the nude scenes, ample time was given to each girl as she shed her clothing, but I was surprised when John appeared. In shot after shot, we were only shown John naked from the waist upwards. In others, we could see that he was naked and prancing about, but the scene was always safely out of focus. At the height of these nudist activities I was stunned to see two shots of myself, fully clothed, gawking in horror at the naked action happening around me. The first was a long shot, and the second a close-up of my face. I didn't look so good in the shot—actually quite ill—and thought that close-up unnecessary. As I sat in his living room, I shifted my eyes in Bolotowsky's direction. He was grinning.

I liked the last scene of the film better. This was the sword fight, and I was surprised and gratified at how dashing I looked in my dueling shirt. To my surprise, the film ended with a close-up of me stabbing John and then looking up at the camera in triumph. (As I remember it, we hadn't filmed those actions in that order.)

After it was over, we all praised the film, and Bolotowsky looked content. "You know," he told us. "I had to play some camera tricks with your friend John. But it had to be done. The reality of the film demanded it."

Like Mailer, Bolotowsky had watched reality going through its dangerous paces. In the end, though, as Bolotowsky and Mailer had both predicted, reality was all in the editing.

II

Ghosts

The Professional Poet

IN A SMALL, intense artistic community like the Hamptons, you probably can't live without making an enemy. And, for a time, I had one. The poet Allen Planz was outraged when he learned that I'd been given the Poets-in-the-schools teaching job. H. R. Hays and Guild Hall's director, Inez Whipple, were in charge of the program. There was money enough to pay one poet at a time at $100.00 per day. Allen had already taught in several schools, and now they'd asked me to continue the program.

Hays explained this to Allen.

It didn't help. Allen needed the money and would scramble for it. He contended that he was the authentic East End poet and deserved the work. He wrote a letter to the editor of the *East Hampton Star*. In it he referred to me as "the poet from down the Island," and invited readers to compare the quality of our poetry by inspecting our books, copies of which could be viewed at the bookstore in town. He predicted that they'd find his poetry superior to mine. He was, he claimed, a "professional poet," while I was something else altogether.

While we were still on speaking terms, Allen and I speculated about whether it was possible to think of oneself as a Professional Poet. At that time, public and private foundations were generous with funds that went to poetry readings and conferences, writing retreats, and educational programs that sent poets into public schools to teach children how to write poetry. The PITS program paid a decent salary for the time. There was a sense that poetry had found its place in American culture, and the poet could survive by writing alone.

Allen, intense, muscular, gruff and ten years my senior, had come to East Hampton from the City in 1967, during the protests against the Vietnam war. He had been part of the anti-war movement, including an anarchist "street gang" called *Up Against the Wall Motherfuckers*, and its offshoot, *The Angry Arts*.

Osha Neumann, founder of the group, described it in Maoist terms: "We saw ourselves as urban guerrillas swimming in the countercultural sea of freaks and dropouts (we didn't like the media term "hippies") who had swarmed to the cheap-rent tenements of the Lower East Side of New York." His group determined to radicalize the freaks and dropouts for "total revolution" through rallies, free feasts and raucous community meetings.

Despite his counter-cultural hostilities, Allen led an ordered literary life. He'd helped organize the reading series at St. Marks Church, and worked for the New York City Department of Parks' Cultural Program.

Then one day, "I said, to hell with it," Allen told me. "The only way to live the life of the professional poet was to get out and live that life."

Robert Bly, the Minnesota poet whose influence on American poetry was felt strongly among the East End poets at the time, once prescribed "one hour in the field for each line of poetry." Planz acted on this, aiming to live in the country and on the surrounding sea as a boat captain and fisherman, from which his poetry would materialize.

The poetry in his first collection, *A Night For Rioting*, reflects contemporary protest anger and the lingering style of the 1950's Beat Generation poets, such as Allen Ginsberg.

In a section of his title poem, he echoes the Lower East Side New York City rhythm:

Ch' ch' d' d' ch ch'
— on a corner, keeping time,
Ready to swing, ready to
make it, stands Cocksman
    Heir to all love's legions.
Tonight he's going to get himself
A party, grab a chick, he's
Going to—dig it!—ball baby ball!
                —"A NIGHT FOR RIOTING"

Later on, though, settled in the East End of Long Island, he allows the rural landscape and the sea to shape his verse:

Once a child built a fortress against the tide.
In darkling sand,
Not to stop it, but to see his craft washed away,
How water touched
To bring all things it touched
To motion,
To flowing
& soon only mounds remain, & nothing within.
                —"SOLSTICE"

"In Rome in the goddam olden days," Allen told me, "poetry was a profession. They had patrons then, the rich people, the nobles and the military officials. They supported the poets imperially. But I can't help siding more with the Russian Communists, like Vladimir Mayakovsky.

He was the best of them; the best of the bad boys. He believed that poetry is work and worthy of compensation. He said, if I make a shoe or I make a poem, what's the difference? Equal work for equal pay."

Allen loved Mayakovsky because he reflected Allen's sense of poetry as revolution. "In our language," Mayakovsky writes, "rhyme is a barrel. A barrel of dynamite. The line is a fuse. The line smolders to the end and explodes; and the town is blown sky-high in a stanza."

Allen was determined to live the ascetic poet's life, but reading and teaching opportunities—the sort of work he imagined should be the poet's lifeline—came to him rarely. To survive, he landscaped, building retaining walls. He worked for a government fish survey program. For several years, he wrote a column for the *East Hampton Star*. Every so often he was invited to read his poetry at venues that paid.

All the while, he dreamed of the sea and a poet-fisherman's life. He began to spend time on the Montauk docks, getting to know the Bonacker fishermen, whose ancestors were the first English colonists in the area. He hired on with them for daytime work, dragging nets in the Atlantic for striped bass and eels. He got to know the Bonackers' variant English, which almost amounted to dialect. He worked with the Baymen, raking oysters and clams and hauled lobster traps out of the water.

Eventually, he had some success as a licensed sea captain, taking paying clients to fish in the deep waters. Finally, he could sail alone as a fisherman-poet out on the ocean.

> ... under the stars, the horizon falling
> Away for miles in stiff cold air,
>   The engine climbing into
>   Full torque
>   And the body singing
> As though wolves howled from extinct caves in the
>   bloodstream.

At our last meeting before Allen's death, we talked again about the old notion of the Professional Poet. In the intervening years, funding for poets and poetry had been reduced to almost nothing. American culture had not admitted the poet into its sheltering womb. Even the Internal Revenue Service had demoted poetry from profession to hobby in the tax code. "No," Allen said. "I don't think it's goddam possible to be a goddam professional poet. You can't live on air. You've gotta eat. You've gotta find a place to sleep."

Meeting Proust's Granddaughter at Canio's, Sag Harbor

CANIO'S BOOKSTORE, A small curiosity shop of crowded shelves on Main Street in Sag Harbor, attracted young writers. You might find anything there. I was in Canio's one day, when I met Marcel Proust's granddaughter.

I'd been attempting to read C. K. Scott Moncrieff's translation of Proust's *Remembrance of Things Past*, off and on since I was sixteen. Now a senior in college, I thought I'd give it another try. Canio's had several volumes of Proust in different editions, and I was whispering to a friend when we were interrupted by a tall, elderly woman.

"I'm standing right here," she said. "And I can hear every word you're saying. So don't say anything insulting about my grandfather."

"Your grandfather?" I said.

"Yes," she said. "My grandfather, Marcel Proust."

This was a striking admission. I didn't know how to respond.

"You're impressed," she said. "I can tell. But I knew my grandfather during the composition of his entire *oeuvre*."

I was excited and wanted to ask her questions, but didn't know where to begin. She continued. "He even posed me as a model for his heroine in the second volume."

"*From a Budding Grove*," I said.

"That's better translated as *Of Flowers and Virgins*."

"You modeled for a novel?"

She smiled modestly. "I was the virgin."

This is where my memory fades. It wasn't too long, however, before I discovered that Proust, once described as a "confirmed bachelor," had neither children nor grandchildren.

I never encountered Proust's granddaughter again, but I remember our meeting as a lovely, lyrical experience. As I've grown older, I've realized that the world is full of ghosts. I've met some of the most interesting in bookstores such as Canio's.

Meeting Capote at Keene's, Southampton

ONE AFTERNOON, WHEN I was in Keene's, a tiny man with a squeaky voice pushed his way through the door, yipping: "Mr. Keene! Who the hell's book is blocking my book in your window?"

The College had recently published my first poetry collection, *Earth Works*, and Keene had given it pride of place, almost entirely blocking another book.

Keene pointed at me. "It's his book."

I knew who the screaming man was; I didn't need an introduction, but Keene introduced us, anyway.

Truman Capote stared at me. "Suppose you tell me, young man, what kind of book you've written that's so damn important it gets to block mine?"

"Poetry," I said.

"Oh," he said, his anger deflating as if poetry threatened nothing. "Hah! Poetry!" he snorted and turned to Keene, beginning a rant about something else.

"Don't take Capote seriously," Keene consoled me later. "He has no respect for poetry, or history, for that matter," he concluded, pointing to a copy of Capote's *In Cold Blood*. "Just you read it. Made the whole thing up. You'll see."

When I returned to Keene's a few days later, the copy of my book that had been in the window was gone. I suspected the worst.

Keene protested, "No, I didn't hide it. It was Capote. After you left, he bought it."

🦃

Keene also published a newsletter called the *Steamboat Press* which he typeset by hand in a shop around the corner. I recall that he published articles about local history, of which he was an expert and the Town's volunteer historian.

One day, he invited me to visit the printshop. Cabinets of type were set against the walls, and a long bedded printing press occupied the center of the room. He showed me how he first inked the form of cold type by turning a crank. The crank caused a roller to impress ink on the type. He then arranged paper on top of the type and, turning another crank, lowered a platen, which pressed the paper against the letters.

I was curious about a stack of type forms standing against a corner wall that extended from floor to ceiling.

"That's my full setting of the original Bible that Johannes Gutenberg published in Mainz," he told me. "Every Latin character as it was originally set. Each page exactly forty-nine lines long. All 973 pages of it."

"How long have you been working on this?" I asked.

"Since I opened the shop twenty years ago. By my calculations, I have twenty more years to go before completing it."

I never heard anything more about this great project. In fact, no one I spoke to who had known Keene could tell me anything about it. Reluctantly, I've come to believe that he had been having fun at my expense, displaying what Sherlock Holmes described as Dr. Watson's "pawkish" sense of humor. It was his joke. He had never set Guttenberg's Bible.

Coffee with Jean Stafford, The Springs

WALKING ALONG SPRINGS Fireplace Road to the bay, I came upon a woman sweeping leaves into a little pile in her driveway. As I passed, I said "Good morning."

She lifted her hand to stop me. "You're the poet staying with the Ignatows?"

Surprised that anyone would know me, I told her, yes, that was true.

"Would you like some coffee?" But before I could answer she said. "Oh. I don't have any coffee."

Each time I met her she was standing at the end of the driveway, wearing her bathrobe. One day she'd smile; another she'd be distracted and wouldn't look at me.

The last time I took that path she was there, dressed formally. "I'm waiting for a car to take me into town," she said. "Very nice to see you."

"Yes," I said. "And to see you, too."

I found out later that she had won the 1970 Pulitzer Prize for her Collected Short Stories, and was getting a ride to Manhattan to accept the award.

Hot and Cold Type: Working for Dan's Papers

URING THE SUMMER after his college graduation in 1961, Dan Rattiner published the first issue of his newspaper, *The Montauk Pioneer*. The newspaper didn't print news, per se; rather it published Dan's topical fantasies and spoofs that had a certain humorous quality—something Richard L. Tobin, then editor of the *Saturday Evening Post* called "fey."

Montauk was Dan's hometown and, because his family owned White's Drug & Dept Store, Dan had grown up knowing the local merchants, to whom he sold advertising. At a later date, Dan had a brilliant idea: He would publish newspapers in most of the East End towns, under different mastheads—*East Hampton Summer Sun, Southampton Summer Day, North Fork Free Enterprise* and so on, using the same editorial content but fresh ads sold to stores in those towns. As much of his Hamptons' readership spent their winters elsewhere, Dan vacationed annually on tropical islands where he would concoct the next season's stories. His winter output, he recalled, was about 70,000 words or the amount contained in a good-sized novel.

Selling local newspaper advertising is difficult, especially when your newspaper is a start-up. By the time I met Dan, he had several ad salespeople covering his territories, all in search of the elusive goal: contract advertising—that is, ads that would run weekly throughout the summer but would only have to be sold once. In search of getting the most out of his Southampton advertisers, he hired me to edit a summer version of the college's weekly, *The Windmill*. I had just completed my junior year and was slated to become editor of the college paper in the fall. Unlike Dan's other papers, this summer insert into the Southampton iteration would publish original stories, which I would write. But it was also my job to sell ads to Dan's Southampton advertisers, from whom he had already culled ads for the paper that enclosed mine.

I was not a talented ad salesman. It was hard going, pleading the neediness of our college paper and emphasizing the community's responsibility to the college, during my sales spiels.

However, I thought I was a good writer.

"No," Dan said. "This story won't work."

"Why not?" I asked.

"It's not funny."

"It's not supposed to be funny," I said. I had written an account of the college's Marine Science program then engaging in nautical exercises on the waters near the college.

A day later, Dan handed me several pages of copy to typeset. (As part of the job, I'd learned to operate his IBM Selectric Composer, which could justify lines of type.) "This is what you should have written," he said. I read over the piece. It was a whimsical satire featuring docile college students depicted as sheep grazing on the campus lawn. "You see. That's funny. Write something funny."

I tried to write something funny, but Dan only took some short, factual paragraphs I'd given him. Instead, he continued filling *The Summer Windmill* with his own work.

Throughout the summer, I tried to imitate Dan's writing style, without much success. Instead of publishing me, Dan found me other work. Because Dan was publishing one of his regional papers every twenty-four hours, there was plenty of trucking and heavy-lifting to do to get the papers distributed.

"I want you to drive this van to Newark, New Jersey—to the Weiss printing plant. Once they do the pressrun, pack up the van and drive it back home. And," he warned. "Be careful of this truck. It's brand new and we've just leased it. No accidents!"

I told him I'd never driven a van before. He told me, blithely, that there was always a first time. He added that the van had a three-speed manual transmission. "Never driven a truck with a stick-shift?" he asked. "There's a first time for everything."

Terrified, I managed to recruit my friend Wendy to come along with me for emotional support. Before we left, Dan handed me a thick manila folder. "Here are a few ads," he said. "Tell Weiss to set them in hot type." (This was at a time when some newspapers were still being set in hot type—liquid lead formed into lines of type by Linotype machine operators, hand-assembled and loaded onto presses.) "These ads won't take them long to set up."

Although there had been much gear-grinding when I first tried shifting, I was able to master the motions. We managed to follow Dan's driving directions, avoiding the parkways that prohibited trucks, and arrived in Newark without mishap.

Mr. Weiss himself met us at the truck bay entrance. "We're running *The Village Voice* now, but your paper is up next.

I gave him the bag of ads and he offered us coffee and sodas in the waiting room. We were beginning to relax when a compositor appeared.

"You gave me thirty ads to set. This will take all night!"

He and Mr. Weiss conferred. The decision was made to put *The Village Voice* on hold and assign the corps of compositors to work on Dan's ads exclusively.

By four in the morning, the van had been loaded with newly print-ed papers. *The Village Voice* was on-press, and we began our drive back to Long Island.

It was eight a.m. when we arrived in Southampton. Because it was a beautiful summer morning, Wendy and I decided to put off return-ing the truck to Dan. Instead, we drove up the road to the ruins of the Scotch Mist Inn, which had been a popular college bar until it burned to the ground. However, in its present solitary decay, it was an equally fashionable place for romantic rendezvous between college students.

If you were reading this story in a Victorian novel, the author at this point might demur further description by suggesting that the curtain of modesty be drawn across the ensuing tender love scene.

However, as Wendy and I found a comfortable spot in the over-grown grass and were just beginning to enjoy the sun and the light breezes of the hilltop, a Suffolk County Police helicopter, like a giant insect from a horror movie, suddenly loomed above the hillcrest, it's loudspeakers roaring. "YOU ARE TRESPASSING ON PRIVATE PROPER-TY! YOU WILL BE ARRESTED!"

Wendy and I ran down the hill to the van. Backing out of the narrow road was difficult, and it became terrifying when the helicopter suddenly bolted toward us. We made it down the hill and onto Route 27A with the helicopter nearly touching the rear of the van. As we accelerated, we heard the loudspeakers roaring: "HA, HA, HA!" —the cops laughing at us, enjoying themselves.

Dan thanked us for finishing the job. He didn't seem surprised that Weiss had had to shunt a big job like *The Village Voice* for our benefit. I told him that I thought I could write a good story about our adventure, but he didn't seem interested.

I spent the rest of the summer selling ads and not being very successful at it. Once, I sold an ad to a restaurant in Hampton Bays. The owner neglected to sign the contract, instead distracting me with a free hamburger. The owner never paid, and Dan had to take the restaurant owner to court to satisfy the bill.

Even so, I learned a great deal about newspaper publishing from Dan, though by the end of that time I'd resigned myself to defeat. Dan hadn't published any of my feature stories. My love-life had been blunted at every turn—once by a police helicopter! To make matters worse, Richard Nixon was president, and I would surely be drafted into the Army in a few months. And in my depression, I wrote a piece—in Dan's style—about the darkness of those times. I invented a term to describe my feelings: "Intellectual Melanism," the idea that my spirit—my whole life—was becoming darkly mottled, opaque. Without hope, I handed the piece to Dan, per-haps only to show him that, while my writing might not have been very good, at least I was trying.

"This is really funny!" Dan said, nodding his head as he read through the piece. "It's really funny! This will go great in the next edition!"

The Art of Lorenzo Parsons

BRIEFLY, IN 1970, I was friendly with a classical painter named Lorenzo Parsons. Although his run-down old house was within a half-mile of de Kooning's newly finished studio in The Springs, East Hampton, Parsons' professed not to know him. "Oh, I've heard of him. Almost knocked him over with my car, bumped him off that rusty bike. Had I done so, it wouldn't have been an accident!"

Parsons, for my edification, ranted about his reasons for having lost all respect for modern painting, especially Abstract Expressionism. "What are they trying to do, these idiots? The last great art movement was French Symbolism. They knew how to paint! They captured image and spirit."

He believed that art was a religion, a polytheistic agglomeration of supernatural oddities. Any art that ignored that realm, he asserted, was sacrilegious. "De Kooning and Pollack. Both degenerates! Atheists!"

He went on: "I was inspired by the great magus, Joséphin Péladan. In Paris when I was young, I witnessed a replica of his last salon, filled with paintings and statues of demonic angels, with women radiating excesses of lust and saintliness, of men of dark power, with the light of merciless heaven in their eyes—all created with the polished, perfected art of the master!" He considered himself an inheritor of Péladan's magic.

One night, after we'd been passing a gallon of Gallo back and forth, he beckoned me to his front yard, where he mounted a stone. "Lo, Jeremiad!" he shouted, waving his arms spasmodically, almost losing his balance. "People of The Springs! I have only to pronounce a certain formula for the earth to open and swallow you all!"

I enjoyed visiting Parsons, who always had some revelation ready to spring on me. His house, reflecting his personality, was curious: a single bedroom, small kitchen and a large, empty room that he called his studio. Oddly, his easel, paints and canvasses were crowded together in the alcove leading to the studio. Everywhere, plaster was hanging from the lathe skeleton within the walls, and you had to walk carefully, lest you fall into the various abysses under the damaged flooring. When I asked why he didn't have the house repaired, he replied that this was a "Holy House of Art." No repairs were needed.

In those years with artists in the Hamptons, I had been immersed in all sorts of modern art, not only paintings, but in the "happenings" created by the dancer and choreographer, Lelia Katayen, the surrealist photography of Val Telberg and in the free-wheeling films of the painter Ilya Bolotowsky. But I was fascinated by Parsons' paintings. To me, they'd come from another world..

"Rembrandt was the last master of light and shade," he said. "He let the artists shelter beneath the black penumbra of his painted shadows without begging attention to their befuddling personal sensibilities."

To me, Parsons' elaborate pictures, painted with thousands of meticulous strokes, were mesmerizing. (Of course, I also believed that my friend, John MacWhinnie, achieved the same startling effect in his paintings with but two or three brushstrokes. This was an opinion I kept from Parsons.)

Every week or so I'd drop into his studio bringing groceries or painting supplies he was too busy to get for himself. But, since doing this allowed me to observe his work habits, I thought it was worth it to me.

One of these habits was obsessive. He'd spend hours on the telephone, having salacious conversations with women who he had to pay for the privilege. It seemed to me that he was spending an awful lot of money in this pursuit. "I'm addicted to it," he said. "Ever since my wife left me, it's all the sex I can get. And it's also the font of my inspiration."

He'd explained what happened with his wife.

Before their marriage, she had been his model—a young student in a painting class he taught for a time at the college. "Supremely versatile. It didn't matter how I dressed her. She always matched the role I was trying to get her to play."

51

He showed me a painting of her on the back of a winged horse, wearing a nun's habit, lightning bolts clutched in her raised hands. Another painting had her emerging from a cave, with an enormous head, eyes sewn shut with ropes, her body transformed into a mammoth serpent.

"These are magical pictures," he said. "Powerful. I dare not show them to the public. There would be riots."

On another occasion, our gallon of Gallo in hand, he showed me nude paintings of his wife. In contrast to the elaboration of the posing model in the first series, these were very simple. Each pictured his wife in the distance of a room, standing or sitting or lying on the floor. The edges of the canvas were shadowed. "It is a keyhole effect," he said. "I got it by painting her while staring through a keyhole." In fact, he confessed, that was the only way he could bear to pose her naked. "Otherwise," he said, "it is just too intense."

He had other paintings to show me. "I'm proud of these, but maybe a little apprehensive," he said.

He explained their origin. "The nude paintings were alright. I really enjoyed peeping at her through the keyhole. But gradually I realized I needed more. So I convinced her to pose for me while having sex with a man. What do you think of that?"

In truth, I didn't and was silent.

"I tried to convince her. 'Art for art's sake, you know', I told her. And after a short period of indecision she agreed. Now the question became, where to find a partner?"

Further east on Springs Fireplace Road was Barnes' Store, one of the few local places at that time where you could get basic food and necessaries. There were several young men who idled around the store, offering themselves for work shoveling snow or mowing lawns in season. Parsons decided to proposition one of them.

He found a boy who agreed to do the job and took him home to meet his wife. To his surprise, his wife and the boy seemed to know each other. "The boy agreed instantly to the modest price I offered. He told me he was ready to get at it. I took my place on the other side of the keyhole. Shortly, my wife and the boy were naked and having sex.

"I was surprised at how much I was enjoying the spectacle," he said. "I could barely take myself away from the keyhole in order to get my paints ready. Well, I was able to convince them to disport for me for almost two weeks, and I painted fourteen pictures. 'Lust On Both Sides of a Keyhole' I call the series."

But at the end of the second week there was trouble.

"That morning, ready to work, I arrived at the keyhole. But the room beyond was empty. I looked around as far as the keyhole would allow, but no one was there. Then I spied a piece of paper taped to the far wall. It seemed to have writing on it. Too timid to enter what had now become for me a chamber out of time and space, a holy, mystical dwelling. I found my telescope and applied the lens to the keyhole. That helped me read the note—really, a farewell letter from my wife. She thanked me for introducing her to the boy. She told me they were planning a journey together. She knew I wouldn't mind if I took the $1,000 I had hidden up the chimney in case of emergencies."

Parsons then looked at me directly. "It may be ironic, but today, I received a letter from the Guggenheim museum. They're putting together an exhibition of Mystical Symbolism. They've invited me to show my work—early middle and late. All of it. They promised to pay me a huge fee and all expenses. The catch is, they will not pay over the money until after the show. I'm left to pay for the trucking of my work to the museum. The irony is that my wife took my last dollars. Do you think you could help me out?"

I was only a college student. A generous cousin had given me a $1,000 to be used for college needs. "How much will it cost to move your paintings?"

"One thousand dollars," he said. "Will you help me out?"

I hesitated.

"If you can see your way clear to the loan, I'll pay you 100% interest the moment the show is over. Come to see me in thirty days. We'll settle up. In the meantime, I'll protect you with my magic blessing," he said, and he raised his arms in a flamboyant gesture that ended with a shimmering descent. "Now, everything will be fine."

I had planned to visit his Guggenheim exhibition, but never saw a notice of the show. Instead, the museum advertised an on-going exhibit of modern work during that month. I stayed away from Lorenzo Parsons' house for the agreed thirty days, anyway, and then decided to visit him.

When I arrived, neither he nor his house was anywhere in sight. I walked around the vacant lot dumbly, as if I expected the house to pop up like a mushroom. One of his neighbors, raking her leaves, came over to tell me that the village had cleared away the wreckage of the house after it had fallen apart during a storm. "It was an eyesore, anyway. They condemned it years ago. But those bureaucrats had to wait for an Act of God before they'd call out the bulldozers."

Some artist friends recalled Lorenzo Parsons as a "character." But to me he was a true magus, whatever else he was. By vanishing before my eyes, taking his house and my money with him, he had given me a demonstration of the kind of dark adult magic I should be wary of throughout my life.

P. G. Wodehouse's Typewriter

W HEN, IN SEPTEMBER of 1966, a day after Labor Day, I found myself decanted onto Main Street in Southampton, near my destination, Southampton College, I was stunned by the post-season silence. Few cars, few people. If I strained, I could hear the ocean a mile and a half away.

Silence was not what I was used to, having spent the previous six years as an adolescent in a military school, sent up the Hudson River near West Point. There, the shouting, head-banging, hazing, blaring military bugles, and my own target practice rifle fire made this sustained silence almost frightening.

There, I had yearned for quiet and found it in the military school library and in recondite places I discovered around campus. The lovely quietude was enhanced by the novels I read, one after the other—or two or three at once—as well as biographies, collections of letters and other literary entries into the lives of the writers who fascinated me.

I found the comic novels of the English writer, P. G. Wodehouse—a momentous discovery. At a library sale, I'd bought several old Penguin paperbacks.

The moment I opened the first I knew I'd come across something wonderful. The title was *Blandings Castle*.

> "Blandings Castle slept in the sunshine," Wodehouse writes. "Dancing little ripples of heat-mist played across its smooth lawns and stone-flagged terraces. The air was full of the lulling drone of insects. It was that gracious hour of a summer afternoon, midway between luncheon and tea, when Nature seems to unbutton its waistcoat and put its feet up."

I loved it: the genteel spreading lawns. The promise of tea and cakes and ices, lawn chairs and hammocks. I knew that there was no world-shaking information to be had here. Rather, I recognized a doorway into something—a summer's afternoon, free of nagging chores—like loading rifles, marching in parades, making my bed, spit-shining my shoes. It was not the real world, I knew. But what was the real world? I was not then ready to commit myself to one thing or another. I recognized in Wodehouse an intimation of immortality. Not the immortal boredom of Heaven, but the comforting immortality of baseball afternoons, when the games without inning limits might go on forever.

In Wodehouse's books I met exquisite people—Jeeves, the omniscient gentleman's personal gentleman, his young master, the addle-pated Bertie Wooster. I come across the doddering Lord Emsworth and his beloved pig, Empress of Blandings, winner of the Shropshire Fat Pigs contest two years in a row. This was delight, itself.

As I read more of Wodehouse, it didn't trouble me that his characters and plots repeated themselves with minor variations. Wodehouse admitted this: "A certain critic," he wrote, "made the nasty remark about my last novel that it contained 'all the old Wodehouse characters under different names'. With my superior intelligence, I have out-generaled the man this time by putting in all the old Wodehouse characters under the same names. Pretty silly it will make him feel, I rather fancy." We both—Wodehouse and I—knew that repetition was beside the point. It was all taking place, as Conan Doyle wrote of his Sherlock Holmes, "in the fairy tale kingdom of Romance."

As a young writer, I began to sense Wodehouse's genius. Intensely interested in the craft of writing, I marveled at Wodehouse's dexterity, seamlessly juggling complex plots, even those narrated by his idiot puppet, Bertie Wooster. While Wodehouse, in the voice of Bertie, manages to tell complex stories, he allows us to laugh at Bertie's naïve follies. I also began to sense a note of cruelty in Bertie's travails.

While outwardly, Wodehouse's stories are constructed of sweetness and light, there is a less visible, darker side shared by don Quixote's creator, Miguel de Cervantes, who enjoyed belly laughs at the frailties and defeats of his idealistic innocent.

In any event, on a family trip to England after my father's death, when I was fourteen, I had hoped to meet the famous author. But a publisher friend of my aunt's told us that Wodehouse hadn't lived in England for years. In fact, he was living in America, on Long Island, in Remsenburg, near Speonk—practically in my own neighborhood!

Back in the States, I looked up his address and wrote to him. He answered in one line, "Sorry. I never knew your father."

But I continued to write. Because I didn't want to bother him, I carefully chose the occasions for writing. Once, a friend in Italy sent a newspaper review of a Wodehouse novel recently translated into Italian. I sent it along to Wodehouse with a note on how odd I'd thought the idea of translating his quaint, comic, quasi-upper-class language into something an Italian reader could relate to. He answered that a friend of his had translated the review, and, in fact, the subject of it was the inexplicable difficulty of a translation that yet could effect a pleasurable result.

I graduated from the military school. I'd discovered other authors who fascinated me, including Marcel Proust, whose multi-volume *Remembrance of Things Past* (now translated as *In Search of Lost Time*) I determined to read in its entirety. (I got about half-way through). But Wodehouse continued to fascinate me. I resolved to meet him in person; the closeness of Southampton to Remsenburg presented an opportunity I couldn't pass up.

I wrote to him, telling him I was now living in his neighborhood. I was thrilled when he wrote back: "You must come around to see me some day. Please call ahead."

I was overwhelmed by his invitation. Without bothering to call, I borrowed a car—a green, 1950 Studebaker Commander, which its owner called "The Avocado"—consulted a map and drove west on Montauk Highway to find his house.

His home was a large, white shingled structure with property that extended down to a creek. "Sometimes," he had written in a letter to a friend, "the creek is at the bottom of the garden. At other times, the garden is at the bottom of the creek."

I found the courage to ring his doorbell. An older woman, his wife, Ethel, I assumed, answered. She told me Wodehouse was not feeling well and couldn't see anyone (not surprising for a man nearing ninety). If I liked, she consoled me, she would give him my regards.

I returned to my dorm deflated. I wondered how I could arrange to meet him.

I fantasized about it and even attempted to write a pastiche in Wodehouse's style. In it, I played the hapless Bertie Wooster, the young idiot who is always saved in the end by his valet, the incomparable Jeeves.

"Jeeves," I told him. "Here is the Grand Plan. In order to meet Mr. Wodehouse I shall employ a simple ruse, or stratagem. I shall follow him in my car as he takes his morning stroll to the local Post Office. 'Good morning, Sir,' I shall say. 'It looks as if it is about to rain.' Then I shall point to the drops of water I've secretly applied to the windshield. 'Why yes,' he will answer. 'Bit of a sticky wicket being stuck in the middle of country without an umbrella.' I then will offer him a ride, which he will accept. 'My word,' he will say as he takes his seat in the front, where he will see I've installed bookshelves, with copies of all his books. 'What an unusual library you have!' he will say. And that, Laddie, will be my cue to unburden myself of the admiration I hold for him. I will show him each of his books, perfectly cared for. He will be moved by my devotion. Perhaps he'll invite me to tea, offer to autograph my copies. Or, possibly he'll read aloud from his newest unpublished novel!"

I awaited Jeeves' praise for my newly displayed brilliance, but the man hesitated, if you can believe it.

"I do not think I would recommend it, Sir," said Jeeves. "It is bound to fail. And, sir, I would not recommend you be seen in public in that, ah, costume."

As was often the case, I had outfitted myself with the gentleman's wardrobe as described by Wodehouse in his stories: Plus-fours, Tam hat, riding boots, floral tie, sunflower in the button hole.

"At least, Sir, abandon the sunflower."

Disappointing, what? But I bucked up, shrugged it off good naturedly. "Don't worry. My Plan cannot fail!"

And then I was off, tootling down the road in the newly resplendent Avocado.

"Well, Sir," Jeeves sighed after attempting to post my bail at the local lock-up. "If you wish to explain how it is that you are now wearing handcuffs after spending the night in a jail cell, I will attempt to resolve the problem to our advantage."

I was, I confess, saddened, rueful—a bit confused. It had all been a misunderstanding (I, told Jeeves, beginning my confession).

My intentions had been honorable. My Plan had started well. I'd come upon Wodehouse walking along, Post Office-bound, supporting himself on a wooden cane. Slowly and quietly I steered the Avocado alongside. "Looks like it's about to rain," I said brightly.

No response from Wodehouse.

I repeated it, louder, but still no reply. Was he deaf?

But no. He turned and looked at me. "What do you want?" he demanded in a most unpleasant tone of voice.

"I want to give you a lift. Keep you dry from the rain."

"There is no rain," said he. "A bright, sunny day! Thanks, but I'll walk."

He continued down the path, getting away from me. What to do? Then a miracle! A clap of thunder, sky darkening. Rain! A sign from Heaven! The car in drive, I caught up. "You see now," I tell him. "It's really raining. You'd better get in the car straightaway!"

"No," he shouted. "I like to walk in the rain!"

Now what? I needed to show him his books on my shelves—my wonderful collection! Books to be autographed! Tea! He, reading aloud to me! I tried again, driving slower, although once nearly hitting him as he tried to cross the road to the dirt path where a car might not go. What to do? Then I saw my chance: A driveway. I turned the Avocado onto the path. (Actually, I noticed in passing, it was not, strictly speaking, a path but someone's wet lawn.) "Mr. Wodehouse," I shouted. "Get in my car this minute. I shan't take no for an answer!" I was concerned for his clothing, you see. Concerned for his health.

Wodehouse looked at me, fear in his eyes. "Get away!" he shouted. "Get away!"

Then in the rearview mirror I saw a police car pull up, leering lights twizzling atop. The cop ordered me to stop, get out of the car, place my right hand on my nose, balance on one leg. "I like to see," the cop said, "the condition of my drivers, Especially when they trespass on private land."

Wodehouse hobbled over to the cop. "This young thug," Wodehouse shouted, his palsied fingers pointing. "This hoodlum is out to kidnap me! See his beady eyes? He must be insane! A lunatic. Look how he's dressed in that clown's costume. Arrest him! Arrest him!"

I abandoned this pastiche. It was not working itself toward a happy ending.

Eventually, I put aside my longing to meet Wodehouse. I had already become friendly with the painters and writers who encouraged my interest in poetry. I'd gone on to better things—more immediate than the satisfaction of a longing to meet a writer whose work I'd studied keenly. Having got to know Ignatow, de Kooning, Bolotowsky and Hays, I came to understand that the artist is not an extension of his or her artwork. It's the other way around—or it's neither. I realized that a blind groping for contact with an artist based only on knowing the artist's work, must end in disappointment. Having served as unofficial chauffeur, therapist, straight-man and witness, to my flesh-and-blood artist mentors, I recognized my infatuation with P. G. Wodehouse as a conceit, the puppy love a young writer develops for an accomplished elder.

In February 1975, I was working on my PhD. while teaching creative writing part-time at Southampton College, and completing the last of the forty workshops I had taught in East End elementary, junior high and high schools. I had learned that Wodehouse was ill and had been taken to Southampton Hospital. He was ninety-four, enfeebled, but still at work on a novel.

On impulse, on Valentine's Day, I drove over to the hospital. I don't know if I actually wanted to see him—to barge into his room to stand by his sick bed—probably his death bed. I believe I only wanted to be quietly nearby, in the vicinity, maybe only to associate myself with the event.

I asked at the desk and was surprised when they gave me directions to Wodehouse's room without any question. I must have been close when I encountered a man and an older woman walking toward me. I thought I recognized Mrs. Wodehouse. I can't imagine that she recognized me. She may have mistaken me for someone else when she motioned to the man next to her who was carrying a suitcase and a typewriter.

"Here," he said. "You can help us with the typewriter."

I understood, then, that I was too late, Wodehouse had died and they were removing his belongings. I accepted the typewriter and followed them into the hospital lobby.

"Put it down here, on top of the suitcase," the man said. "The car will be around in a minute."

"Thank you," Mrs. Wodehouse said to me.

I offered a smile, turned and waved as I walked rapidly away.

I knew that if I'd stayed a moment longer I'd invite suspicion about who I was and why I was there—questions I would be too embarrassed to answer. In any case, I'd gotten as close to meeting Wodehouse as a naive young writer could have at that moment: I had carried his typewriter.

III

Communists In The Hamptons
Stuffing Ideology Into Art

"WE WERE ALL Communists back then," H. R. Hays said. "All the poets and artists." He noticed my silence. "Well, don't look so shocked. Besides, I suppose yesterday's Communists are today's Democrats; there's really little difference. It was the only thing to be in the 1930's. When you witnessed the mistreatment of the workers, the minorities—and anyone else who wasn't a wealthy white man—there was really no other choice."

"Did they ever put you in jail?" I asked.

"No," he said. "Somehow they missed me, even though I gave them plenty of ammunition."

In the early 1960s, middle-class Americans would have been terribly shocked if someone they knew in our rigid, fiercely buttoned-down society admitted to being a Communist. Condemnation was swift then, if not as outright hysterical as it had been in the 1950s. The Vietnam War, which was growing more all-consuming by the day, was on the surface a war against Communism. Yet, with the number of casualties multiplying and the accusations of government cover-ups and corruption, the actual menace of Communism itself, if it existed at all, was for us college students, only a vague, irrelevant concern.

But I shouldn't have been so surprised at Hays' Communist confession. In a unique place like the Hamptons, residences of the very wealthy, the workers who supported them, and multiple economic and artistic strata in-between—not to mention a significant portion of the population that was absent for the darker months of the year—I shouldn't have been shocked to find Communists thrown into that mix.

By the time I'd gotten to know H. R. Hays, David Ignatow, Willem de Kooning and Ilya Bolotowsky, they had all dealt with Communism in various ways (some joining the Party, others not) and had resolved those issues they might have had with the challenge of Socialist Realism in art. In the end, they had rejected it because they found it unworkable.

The reason for their rejection was obvious, even to me. The four tenets of Socialist Realism that Maxim Gorky had laid down in 1932—that art must be relevant to workers, that it portray typical scenes of everyday life, that it be representational, not abstract, and that it be supportive of the aims of the Party—presented a challenge to painters and writers, that they must somehow incorporate Communist ideology into their work. To try to follow these dicta was ultimately as contrary to the temperaments of the Hamptons' artists as doing paint-by-numbers portraits of landscapes filled with happy little trees.

Take Jackson Pollock, for example. Explosive and withdrawn, he had escaped the encroaching city and with his wife, Lee Krasner, would move to The Springs in 1945. Pollock came from a large family of actual, card-carrying Communists and Communist sympathizers—the so-called "fellow-travelers" that Senator McCarthy and his henchman, Roy Cohn, would repeatedly smear decades later. In 1939, with the encouragement of his older brother, Charles, Pollock moved to New York City and became a student of Thomas Hart Benton at the Art Students League. Soon he abandoned Benton's regionalist apolitical pictures for an allegiance with modernist art infused with politics. He was most interested in the Mexican muralists, Surrealism, and Picasso, especially Picasso's *Guernica*. He believed with Diego Rivera that "art is propaganda, or it is not art."

His break from Benton, who had watched sadly as his students turned their art to leftist causes, led him into a long period of internal struggle. In 1940, he wrote to his brother that "I have been going through violent changes the past couple years. God knows what will come out of it all—it's pretty negative stuff so far." Much of that time he had been testing the assumption that political ideas could not only be subjects for paintings, but could be infused into the fabric of the paintings themselves. Eventually, he gave it up and turned to the free-form Abstract Expressionist works for which he is now known.

Unlike Pollock, Ilya Bolotowsky, who had been born in Russia and was a teenager during the Revolution, had not been even remotely a Communist. Despite this, he encouraged me to listen to old '78 records featuring, among other works, "Iron Foundry," a relic of the Russian Revolution. "Iron Foundry," Bolotowsky explained, is the famous piece of the composer Alexander Mosolov and a prime example of Soviet futurist music. It was an attempt to make a music truly for the people, with sounds that the Russian worker would instantly recognize. In fact, I discovered, these disks were recordings of the unrelenting clangs, bangs, and whistles, the deafening noises of factory machines imitated by musical instruments. As far as I know, the history of this grotesque artform remains—and should remain—buried in those old '78s.

Ironically, the louder H. R. Hays proclaimed himself a Communist, the less the government paid attention to him. In 1934, he joined the Artists' Union, which had just been formed. Its mission was to find work for unemployed artists—an ideal, if not a practical undertaking at the time since the union had no leverage. However, the next year, President Roosevelt supplied it. He issued an Executive Order, later funded by Congress, establishing the Emergency Relief

Appropriation Act. From this, the Works Project Administration was created. Among its mandates, the WPA was tasked with supporting the public works of artists. The Artists' Union immediately set itself up as the artists' advocate, lobbying for more jobs within the Works Progress Administration, better pay and working conditions, and against proposed cutbacks. Essentially, the Artists' Union became the mediators between artists and WPA, settling grievances between workers and bosses and threatening to take direct action if needed.

Hays, Harold Rosenberg and their writer and painter friends, such as de Kooning and a reluctant Mark Rothko, joined the union.

At the time, Hays definitely considered himself a writer, and was at work on a novel. In early middle age, he was a strikingly handsome man, as a photograph by Alfred Eisenstaedt published in LIFE magazine showing him in the stacks of the New York Public Library, reveals. He had made friends with Rosenberg and his wife, May. Rosenberg, who would later famously characterize the methods of Willem de Kooning, Jackson Pollock and others as "action painting," had trained as a lawyer, but after an illness that forced him to walk with a cane for the rest of his life, gave up the law for a Bohemian lifestyle in East Hampton and New York City and a devotion to writing poetry. May Rosenberg, a teacher and social worker, introduced Hays to a university art student named Juliette Levine. They got on and married in New York City Hall in 1934.

Juliette Hays described a typical artist-union action of the time. The word, she told me, would go out to all the projects—dancers, writers, artists—of a sit-in that was planned. After a performance, the cast members would ask the audience if they would join the sit-in with them. Outside, they were met by other theatre people, as well as the artists, poets and writers who were working on other projects. It was the rule that no one would re-enter the theater while the protest was in progress. "So mostly," she said, "there were writers and some dancers outside and we were marching back and forth. We were shouting slogans. It made a powerful sound when you had several hundred people with you. We looked back (at least I did) to Broadway. And suddenly coming around the corner, these banners appeared. They were Artist Union banners and Marcus [Mark Rothko] was carrying a banner and he was on the line."

Aside from sit-ins and marches, Hays' Marxism rested in the realm of ideas, and his actions for the cause were more literary than street-revolutionary. Intellectuals and artists had a recognized place in the social reform movement of that time, and Hays contributed regularly to such Socialist magazines as *The New Masses.*

Along the way, Hays formed a relationship with the German playwright, Bertolt Brecht, whom he sponsored for entry into the U. S. when Brecht fled the Nazis. Hays has described Bertolt Brecht's significance to German and world literature as arising from the fact that his philosophy molded his style and dictated the forms in which he worked.

Hays' attempts at poetry for the Marxist cause employed the familiar vocabulary and ideas of working class solidarity with muted Imagist or Surrealist shadings. For example in "Parade" published in the *New Masses* he wrote:

> Thinking of May Day when
> Continents rush together
> And there is only one sky ....
>
> ...
>
> Thinking of May Day,
> Of parades
> Moving like history,
> Those in back
> Must run to keep up—
> The vanguard Marches in Moscow.

Hays wrote several of these propaganda poems attempting to fuse politics with art. Whether he thought he had succeeded or not is evidenced by the fact that none of them showed up in his later poetry collections.

In his theatre work, Hays collaborated with Bertolt Brecht and Hanns Eisler, both passionate Communists, both investigated by the U. S. Congress, who made at least public attempts while in the U. S. to "rehabilitate" themselves, to seem to become good Americans. These attempts failed, and both eventually were forced into exile. Another Hays collaborator—and, famously, Brecht collaborator—was Kurt Weill. Soon after settling in New York, Weill, paired with Hays on Hays' Broadway musical, *The Ballad of Davy Crockett*. Weill, too, was a Marxist who tried to rehabilitate himself by nestling into mainstream American theatre. Unlike Brecht and Eisler, Weill was successful.

Hays' work for the Federal Theatre Project, especially as author and administrator of the *Living Newspaper* series, might have brought him to the attention of the Dies Committee, a forerunner of the House Un-American Activities Committee, whose purpose was to permanently end subversive public works—such as the Federal Theatre Project. During the four years of the Project's existence, the government harassed several productions. One play, Marc Blitzstein's *The Cradle Will Rock*, was notably closed down on opening night by armed federal troops. It was inevitable that the Dies Committee should step in and initiate an enquiry. Despite the literary historical ignorance of Committee members leading the inquiry (much time was wasted trying to ascertain whether the 16th century British playwright Christopher Marlowe, was now or had ever been a Communist), the government finally shut down the Federal Theatre program.

Still, the government hadn't noticed Hays. And that didn't change even with the 1938 production in Madison Square Garden, of Hays' *A Song About America*, a tribute to Vladimir Lenin and the 20th anniversary of the October revolution, with music by Eisler. "They got a real file on me then," Hays said.

One of the songs from the play, "Sweet Liberty Land," became very popular and was for some time the unofficial national anthem of the Communist Party of America. "It almost replaced the 'Internationale,'" Hays told me.

Eisler, fearing deportation, had written his music under the pseudonym "John Garden." Despite this precaution, he was discovered and deported.

But Hays, who had boldly refused to use a pseudonym as author of this radical production, was never called before any government committee.

This annoyed him. "They ignored me," he sniffed.

In a limited way, Hays had been successful stuffing Stalinist ideology into words and music for a small audience. But as times changed, so did the way people reacted to Hays' work. By 1982, when Guild Hall in East Hampton commenced an ambitious experiment that accidentally echoed a strain of Socialist Realism, Hays was well known as a playwright, a poet, and a pioneer of early television drama. Guild Hall invited Hays, me and eighty-two others to collaborate on this experiment, the *Poets and Artists* exhibition.

It was not a collaboration without precedents. In Russia, shortly before and after the Revolution of 1917, the partisans of Socialist Realism had not always been of the proletariat. Some of the Futurists made comfortable bourgeoise livings by obeying the artistic whims of their Capitalist masters. And so, on a balmy summer day, an echo of this relationship between artists and the wealthy manifested itself in East Hampton.

That summer, Guild Hall invited poets and artists to participate in the show organized by Lillian Braude, wife of Quadrangle Books (now Times Books) publisher and poet Michael Braude. Mike provided the money, as well as a poem for the show.

The idea for it had been suggested by the painter Jimmy Ernst, son of the German Surrealist master, Max Ernst. Jimmy had developed a distinct collaborative style, marrying abstract, crystalline form to spirituality, influenced by jazz and Native American culture. The idea that poets and painters could work together, combining their creative instincts and art forms seemed a natural pairing to him. And why not? The climate was right. Only recently, free-form Happenings had been staged in arts venues in the Hamptons. These were improvisations involving artists from different fields and people who had just happened to walk in off the streets and were recruited to play a part.

Lillian Braude wrote in her Introduction to the exhibit catalog: "Our painters are well known. But our poets live more private lives, and one aim of this exhibition is an attempt to give them greater exposure." Rose Graubart and David Ignatow contributed an essay beginning with a Chinese maxim: "Poetry is a picture without form, and painting is a poem without form" in order to underline the alleged inevitability of the successful pairing of poets with painters.

Forty-two painters and forty-two poets were asked to participate. The only rule laid down by Guild Hall was that a poem, or section of a poem, had to be incorporated into the painting.

For the poets who got in early to make their choices, each was able to select a painter friend with whom they'd had a long acquaintance. Judging by the results, their collaborative experiences produced art that was natural and fresh. One especially pleasing work was titled "Revenge," created by Willem de Kooning and Harold Rosenberg.

But for others, poets who came late to the selection process who had to choose from artists whose work they may not have known, the collaborations and their results were mixed.

My partner in the collaboration was David Porter, whom I had met only a few times in connection with his real estate business. I didn't know his paintings, and he didn't know my poetry. After he'd read through my work, he told me that he hadn't found a single poem that moved him. He apologized that he wasn't familiar with the modern, free verse style in which I was writing. We discussed it, and finally agreed to use two lines to inspire the painting. I think the result was good, in spite of everything. The painting was titled "Under the light/ of the first falling snow."

Apparently, we were among the lucky ones of that latter group. We heard whispers of artistic temper tantrums, shouting matches and even a fistfight. For some, the major obstacle to success was that their individual visions were at odds with each other. One painter so loathed his poet-collaborator's work that, once the exhibit was done, he tore off the paper glued to the painting, on which his collaborator's poem had been written, and exhibited the picture as a stand-alone with a different title, absent any credit to the poet.

Even so, most agreed that *Poets and Artists* had been at least an entertaining experiment. In the end, none of the collaborators had abandoned the project. The cocktail and dinner parties that followed were the kind of excessive and wonderful experiences that the Hamptons are known for. Guild Hall put on a generous and celebrity-studded opening night reception. Michael and Lillian Braude followed with a party at their home in the toniest East Hampton neighborhood.

That party was memorable for its abundance of exquisitely prepared hors d'oeuvres, meats and fish, and for its unending river of alcohol, all served by uniformed waiters who never stopped circling throughout the rooms. The Braudes invited us to wander through their home. We were flabbergasted by the Picassos, Monets and other French Impressionists hanging on the walls.

It was the exception and not the rule that attempts to shove ideology into art, whether by Communists or Capitalists, produced anything that was great or lasting—witness the attempts by Pollock, Hays and other Hamptons artists. But for the non-political artists and poets attending the party at the Braude's, there seemed a quicker way to resolve the question: a corkscrew, liquor, and lots of ice.

IV

Robert, in Twelve Episodes

1. The Feral Poet

IN THE FALL semester of my junior year at Southampton College, I was lucky enough to get a part-time job house-sitting. House-sitting required a student to spend each night, from six in the evening to six in the morning, in one of the large Hamptons summer homes that had been abandoned for the winter, their owners and families migrating to warm places such as Palm Beach or the South of France. Our mission was to protect the houses from intruders.

I was disappointed with my assignment. Instead of a house in Southampton near the college, mine was located way out in The Springs, at the end of Springs Fireplace Road in East Hampton, about a forty-minute car trek from my dorm.

The house was an old wooden clapboard, designed (so my instruction sheet told me) by the architect Edward Purcel Mellon some time in the early 20th century. It had porticos for horse carriages on each side, a long porch (called the Front Porch) on the rear of the house facing Gardiner's Bay and a tower with a widow's walk. It didn't take me long, after I'd dropped my bag off in a bedroom next to the kitchen, to discover that the fall wind that sledded over the bay, swirled around unchecked inside the house, encountering little resistance from the loose and uninsulated clapboards of the exterior. It must be a pleasant place in the summer, I thought, when the breezes wafted from Gardiner's Island. But cold as hell in the winter.

My job was to alert the police to any break-ins. I tried the doors off the kitchen, but they were locked. I hadn't been told where to locate the keys. With only the kitchen, bedroom and a small bath open to me, I didn't think I'd be much help if anyone got in into another part of the house through a window. In any case, with the Labor Day departure of tourists and the exodus of the wealthy, the chance of the house being burglarized seemed remote. The only people left in town were the indigenous folk, called Bonackers, who supplied maintenance services to the big homes. They all knew each other and kept their eyes on any stranger visiting in town.

But an incident in my second week on the job proved that I was wrong. At around eleven o'clock one night, I was doing my homework, when I heard a noise. It was not the wind rattling the windows, but a series of seemingly random taps and scratches coming from the window next to the front door.

The lights were out in the kitchen. Like a blind man in a cartoon with my arms extended and bumbling against the walls, I made my way toward the noise.

Careful to stay in the shadows, I got close enough to the window to confirm that there was, indeed, a tall, thin, awkward male perpetrator wearing a backpack, trying to pry open the window with what I took to be a spoon. He didn't seem to be getting anywhere.

I was about to sneak back to the kitchen to telephone the police, when the moonlight caught his face and made him recognizable. It was a guy I knew, a fellow student in one of David Ignatow's poetry writing classes named Robert.

I threw open the front door. "Robert!" I said. "Can I help you with something?"

"Oh," he said. "Well, I suppose it would have been easier to knock on the door. May I come in?"

"Hmm. I guess you can."

"I looked for my key—house key, you see—but couldn't find it. Maybe I never had it. Anyway, I couldn't find it."

"Why would you have a house key?"

"Why? Why shouldn't I? I mean, this is my family's house."

I was surprised but prepared to take him at his word.

"What a cold place this is," he said, throwing his backpack into a corner by the old barrel-chested porcelain sink. "I never lived here much. But I know where everything is."

He opened a wooden cabinet door in the kitchen and found a bunch of keys. He selected one and opened the locked door into the living room. "My father kept multiple sets of keys, so he'd never get shut out of the house, no matter how late the night and how drunk he was."

He switched on lights. We walked across the dusty carpet into the dining room. There was a long table with chairs and place settings under a crystal chandelier.

"Have you eaten?"

I told him I'd had a sandwich I'd brought with me.

"No. That won't do. I'm hungry. Sit down at the table. Let me see what I can find."

He left for the kitchen. I heard him fussing with drawers. He returned with a tray on which were several items.

"I don't know what you'll like. Do you like Dinty More Beef Stew? It's one of my favorites. Just open the can, dump it into a pot and heat it up. Delicious! And here's this canned spaghetti. That's easy to make. Oh, and I found this in the refrigerator. I thought you might be interested in it. I myself can't stand the stuff."

It was a half-kilo jar of Ossetra caviar. "This was left over from the summer. I don't suppose it's still good. Do you like the stuff?"

I'd heard of caviar but had never tasted it. This batch looked like it could poison someone.

"And I've got some cold beer. There's plenty of whiskey, too. Some-where. My father always has bottles hidden everywhere. Here's something, a bottle of Scot's Mac—wine and whiskey mixed together. Ugh! Here's a can of sausages. I can heat them up for us. And there's plenty more in the pantry. In fact, there are several pantries. We can explore them together. We can have a real feast!"

He had convinced me. This was his parents' home, I was sure. In any case, I was realized I was hungry, too. "Go ahead," I said. "Let's have a feast."

We drank beer and ate the canned stew. Robert began to shovel the food into his mouth. After a while he put down the spoon and began rapidly picking the chunks of meat and vegetables out of the bowl with his fingers. He was enthusiastic and licked his bowl when there was only gravy left in it.

"You know," Robert said as we sat around on the living room couches after dinner. "This reminds me of *Bertie's Escapade*, a book my mother read to me when I was very young. I memorized it. It's all about a pig named Bertie. 'It was twelve o'clock on a winter's night,' the story begins. 'The fields, the hedges were covered with snow. The only dark spot in the paddock was Bertie the Pig.' Yes, indeed," Robert said. "Bertie was a pig of action. Deeds, not grunts, was his motto. One December night he and his friends go Christmas caroling at Mr. Stone's—certain they will be invited in afterward to enjoy a splen-did supper. And so they begin an evening that turns out to be much more of an adventure than Bertie had anticipated. Much like tonight with us here," Robert said, smiling. "Who knows what this night will bring?"

Then, abruptly, his eyes rolled, his lids closed and he was asleep. I left him there on the couch.

My alarm rang at 6 am. I had an early class. Robert was still asleep on the living room couch, but opened his eyes as I approached.

He smiled. "That was a lovely feast we had, wasn't it? I dreamed we'd gone carol singing with Benjy the Rabbit and the other animals. *Bertie's Escapade.* I love that book!"

I asked him where he'd parked his car.

"I don't drive," he said. "I hitchhike everywhere. It stirs my poetic imagination."

I offered him a ride in my car.

"Ah-ha!" he said when he saw it. "It's the Avocado. I recognize it."

The so-called Avocado, a 1953 Studebaker painted avocado green was owned by another student, who loaned the car to any of us for a small fee.

We drove into East Hampton Village. I wanted coffee, so we stopped at Speed's restaurant. I liked Speed's because Joseph Heller, the author of *Catch-22*, was often there. He wasn't there that morning.

A man was walking out of the café as we were walking in. At the sight of him, Robert turned his face away. The man left without looking at us.

"That's my shrink," Robert said. "He shoots me up with Ritalin to make me talk. Each of our sessions last three hours. It's exhausting."

"Why did you turn away from him?"

"We're not on speaking terms."

I didn't see Robert during that day. After my last class, I drove the Avocado back to the house in The Springs. Robert greeted me at the door.

"I think I'll stay here for a while, if you don't mind. We can be roommates."

It was lonely by myself in this remote house every night, so I welcomed the idea.

2. The Evidence

WHEN WE WEREN'T working on our academic assignments, Robert filled the evenings with his stories. Even without Ritalin injections, he loved to talk.

One day he pointed to his knapsack and said: "I've been carrying this thing around for a long time. This thing is significant. In here is the very important evidence."

"Evidence of what?"

"The pieces of the puzzle. One lucky day, I'll dump them on the floor and they'll fall into place.."

"What puzzle?"

"My life," he said. "The evidence about the puzzle of my life. Let me show you."

He set the case down and flipped the latches. The inside was stuffed with books, party masks, rubber balls and what might have been a fossilized baloney sandwich. Robert pulled out a folder.

"I'll give you an example. These are my elementary school teachers' evaluations of me, year by year. Here's from third grade arithmetic: 'While almost all the solutions to problems in his notebook are wrong. Robert has yet a fair understanding of the work we have done this year and has grasped the steps involved.'"

He pulled out another. "'I don't believe Robert considers the descant recorder to be a real musical instrument. If he did he could play it.'"

He shuffled some more.

"Now, here's one that shows you the mean person that Mrs. Stuttgart really was. This one's from Fourth grade: 'Robert likes to go through the motions of work—with impressive speed. He sits down to a page of writing with the air of an executive who, at the end of the day at his office, is about to sign the stack of outgoing letters. His own writing, then, is in character: an undecipherable scrawl. His pretense and evasion of responsibilities have to be exposed to him almost daily.' Maybe she thought she was being too hard on me. She finished up by writing: 'Yet he is happy and full of virtue when he has been made to work well.'"

Robert looked up at me, awaiting a reaction.

"I don't think she's so much mean as sarcastic. Defensive, really."

"Well, she did have some insight. Listen to this, about gardening: 'Honest physical work is distasteful to Robert and he did as little as possible.'"

"Yes. She got you on that one."

"But here's one that actually makes sense: 'Robert is constantly beset by distractions, many of them of his own fabrication. He has often to be stopped from pouring forth an almost constant stream of muttered comments, unrelated to the lesson.' How about that one?"

"That really happened? It sounds as if you had some issues there."

"Maybe so. But I remember exactly what I was doing. I told you I always wanted to be a writer, even at that young age, to tell stories? That's what I was doing. Telling stories about the kids in the class, about the adults in the school, and about Mrs. Stuttgart, too."

"And you think that that was all fine and normal?"

"Think about it." Robert said. "Real life is nothing but a bunch of disconnected actions. They don't make sense. What you need is a storyteller, a poet to pull them together. And that's what I've always been. The one who writes the poem, the one who tells the story about it all."

3. Teen Angel

"You just don't know what 'love-sick' means," Robert was telling me after dinner one night, "unless you've spent your boyhood in all-boys prep schools."

Robert's parents had shifted him from one school to another—from a Quaker-themed progressive school, where the boys learned to knit and crochet, to a kind of medieval English public school, where the boys took freezing cold showers and learned to torture each other.

"Each time Mom or Dad got divorced, they'd get me away from their emotional thunderstorms by plucking me out of one school mid-year and parachuting me into another.

"As I said," Robert went on, "these were all-boys schools. None of us, as we grew up, knew anything about girls. I mean, how did you meet a girl? What did you say to her? What was a good pick-up line? What did you do on a first date, or a second date—and how did you do it?

"In one school I discovered something that helped keep me going.

"There was a biology instructor, an old man who had been teaching there forever. His classroom was crowded with all sorts of weird things, including some specimen jars with mummified frogs, birds, squirrels and other animals," Robert said. "But the jar I found astounding was the one in which there was a human head floating in formaldehyde.

"It was a head that had been cut in half, from the top of the scalp down to the neck. From one angle you could see the cross-section of the brain, the empty nasal passages, the nose, and the mouth. But the real shock was what you could see when you turned the jar around.

"It was a real person's head—a girl's head—with wisps of blond hair down to her ear. She had a pert nose and pretty lips. Her eye was closed. (If it had been open, I think I would have fainted.)"

"Did your teacher tell you who she was or how she got to be that way?"

"No. We never asked. Somebody found the jar in a cabinet. We thought the teacher was hiding it. Or maybe he only showed it to his older students.

"Anyway, I couldn't take my eyes off her. I'd sneak a peek into the cabinet after school or between classes. At first, I looked at both sides of her head. The dissected side was so anonymous, so brutally ugly, while the other side was soft. A soft, pretty girl about my age."

"Eventually, I only wanted to look at the human half." He paused to savor the memory. "That's when I began to fantasize about her."

"What do you mean?" I asked. I wasn't sure where Robert's story was going, nor whether I wanted to hear the rest of it.

"I built her a life history. I imagined she'd died young from some incurable disease or foolish accident. There was a song on the radio back then, *Teen Angel*, about a girl who's car stalls on a railroad track. Her boyfriend pulls her out to safety, but she runs back and the train mows her down. The boyfriend is heartbroken. He wants to know: *'Teen angel, can you hear me? Are you somewhere up above? And I am still your own true love?'* Really sorrowful, right?

"Anyway, at some point I decided that her name was Jennifer, and that she was my girlfriend. We had lots of dates and went to movies and her school dance together."

"Oh, come on," I said. "You didn't really, did you?"

"Well, I didn't know other girls," Robert said. "I fantasized about her so much. Maybe I should have talked to the school chaplain or doctor or someone about it. But, really, things were going along okay for us."

Robert paused, his eyes closed, a smile on his lips. I suspected he was getting ready to deliver the punch line.

"I tell you, I really loved Jennifer, I did. The trick was to look at her only on the good side of the jar. If you turned the jar to her other side…. Well," he said, "she'd just break your heart."

4. Family History

ROBERT HAD BEEN showing me around the house and grounds, pointing out different things he thought would interest me.

"Captain Cook, the pirate, buried his treasure somewhere around here, maybe across the water, on Gardiner's Island. When I was a kid I used to row over there and look for it," Robert said.

I knew that a descendant of the Gardiner family lived on the Island and was not partial to treasure hunters.

"That was Robert David Lion Gardiner. He never bothered me. He was great friends with my father. They used to get drunk together."

Something had been on my mind and I posed it to Robert: "Most of the big places kids from the college house-sit," I said. "They're in the wealthier sections. I mean, right in there with all the big houses. But your house, out here by itself in The Springs. What's the story with it?" I really wanted to know something about his family but didn't know quite how to ask.

Robert understood. "It was my mother's family that had the money. My father, when he met my mother, was only a poor movie star."

Of course, this intrigued me. "A poor what?"

"Yes. Movie star, in the 1940s. You see, my father was a good looking man, but an odd duck, as he often called himself," Robert said. "He let his good looks take him anywhere that promised pleasure. He told me he didn't recall exactly how he'd become an actor. One day, he said, he found himself on a Broadway stage, dressed as a cowboy. 'Cowboy Number Two', his role was. He had only one line: 'We used to ride the range with a bunch of steers, now we ride with a bunch of dudeens'— by which was meant 'female dudes'. The show was a success and ran for several years. My father recited his line at every performance. When he got tired of it, he changed 'dudeens' to 'dudettes', just for the variety."

The show, Robert said, moved on to Hollywood for filming with Mickey Rooney in the starring role. My father's photo began to appear in fan magazines. Young girls—Bobbysoxers—wrote him love letters. They demanded to see him in more films. "The problem was, as my father was the first to admit, he couldn't really act," Robert said.

"The studios cast him in roles that didn't demand too much from him. I remember he played a corpse in a Humphry Bogart film, and posed for the portrait in *The Picture of Dorian Gray*. All he had to do was hold still.

"His big break came when he auditioned for the lead in *Gone With the Wind*. He did screen test after screen test, reading lines with the actresses who were vying to play Scarlett O'Hara. Eventually, his part was given to Clark Gable, who really could act. Meanwhile, he'd met and married my mother.

"She was from a family that lived in Southampton on Dune Road by the Atlantic Ocean during the warm, lighter parts of the year. When she brought my father home, she found that her family didn't approve of him. They didn't like actors. So, at their direction, my parents pretty soon got divorced. He ended up with this house far away from Mother's family, in this wild spot. This house was his separation gift, I suppose."

Robert paused thoughtfully, then continued: "I'd already been born. For a while, my parents passed me back and forth. Sometimes I lived in Southampton; other times out here. Then, from age six on, it was boarding schools all the way down.

"So, you see," he said. "Art courses through my veins. At least, one side of my veins."

"What courses through the other side?" I asked.

"Money, I suppose. It's always there in the background. A cushy chair tempting me to sit in it and throw away my bardic dreams."

87

5. Eating Gold

ONCE, WHEN ROBERT was ten or eleven, at home on vacation from one of his boarding schools, he found his father in the kitchen, a bottle of Scotch by his side, plunging a soup spoon into a large jar and thrusting the contents into his mouth. What he was gorging looked like orange marmalade or even tiny orange ball bearings. "I've found it," Robert recalled his father shouting. "It's Captain Kidd's treasure!"

How could you eat gold? The young Robert wondered.

"It's not exactly gold, but it's worth its weight in gold, me hearty!"

Robert watched his father in the role of a pirate, flourishing his soup spoon cutlass.

His father waited expectantly for Robert to ask him what it was he was eating. But Robert stayed quiet, fascinated by the image of his swashbuckling father.

"It's caviar," shouted his father impatiently. "But not any caviar. This is the golden caviar of the sterlet sturgeon. The rarest and most expensive in the world. Worth its weight in gold, I tell you—or better! Try a spoonful!"

Robert hesitated but took the big helping of golden eggs and sniffed. It smelled of the sea, salty. "Eat it! Consume it!" his father ordered.

Robert slid the spoon into his mouth and delicately licked the caviar off. His first reaction was surprise. It was as if the tiny eggs were exploding on his tongue. The taste was of fish, which he didn't particularly like.

"Have another spoonful," said his father.

Robert put it into his mouth. Same thing: Explosions. Fishy taste.

"Well," said his father noting the sour face Robert made. "There's really only enough here for me. Go eat some ice cream."

"This whole caviar thing started when my father married Franzi," Robert said. Franzi was his father's third or possibly fourth wife.

"She knows everything about that muck and seduced my father into it. And it didn't stop there. He let her have her way, and she got him eating foie gras, truffles, snails, every other kind of mollusk—you name it. She was trying to make him a gourmet. And she succeeded, wildly."

In fact, under her tutelage, he'd become a rhapsodic glutton.

"The last straw for me," Robert said, "was coming home for a visit. No one seemed to be in the house, but then I heard noises in the kitchen. They were all in there: Franzi, the cook and two maids. My father was there, too, in a high chair, his arms and legs strapped by leather belts to the arms and legs of the chair, a linen napkin draping his head."

Robert asked Franzi what was going on. She was moving around the kitchen with a cage of small birds that fluttered helplessly.

"Franzi said that they were preparing for my father's initiation into gourmet society. These little birds were Ortolans. For hundreds of years, a rite of passage for gourmets was eating the Ortolan. 'Eating them alive?' I asked. 'No,' she said. 'First we drown them in Armagnac, then we roast them whole.' 'What do you do with all the guts and bones?' I asked. "Nothing," she said. "We eat the little birds—bones, guts, feathers and all.'"

"I tell you," Robert told me. "I was revolted. And all the time my father was sitting there with a silly grin on his face. I said to Franzi 'What's the meaning of the linen napkin on his head?'

"'Well,' Franzi said. "It's to preserve the precious aromas. Of course, some people believe it is also there so that the gourmet may hide his face from God.'"

Franzi had been born in a German Canton of Switzerland. Her first husband had died when a human body fell on him as he was hiking near the Reichenbach Falls. "They're always throwing themselves off those high rocks," Franzi said.

Her second husband had died of natural causes in Geneva, as had her third. There was nothing suspicious about her widowhood, Franzi assured Robert. Just bad luck.

To break this cycle, Franzi took an ocean liner to America. It was a mid-winter crossing, and the ship was caught in an ice storm. "The water was leaking through the portholes. Everyone on my deck was vomiting."

Robert imagined her trapped below decks, in steerage. "Couldn't you move up to a better cabin?"

"There was no up. Mother and I were in First Class. After all, my father owned the cruise line."

Along with money from her father, each of her husbands had left Franzi an inheritance, so she was free to live anywhere. She chose The Springs. She bought land deep in the woods and started construction of what she called a typical Swiss chalet. "I wanted to build a mountain, too, or at least a hill, to make a ski slope, but the village wouldn't give my builder the permit."

One late October afternoon, Robert's father had got lost on his weekly walk in the woods and ended up at Franzi's new chalet. "I took him back to his home and, of course, we fell in love and married."

Robert, who was away at school, missed the details of his father's new marriage. He didn't hear from them again until his school's headmaster called him into his office. "Your father has taken ill. You're to go home."

Robert was surprised when he saw his father. Rather than looking the part of the terminally ill patient, his father was seated on the sofa in his dressing gown drinking champagne. Robert marveled at how well he looked. He must have lost fifty pounds.

"You see," said Franzi. "That's the problem. The weight loss. It's one of his symptoms. He says he's bloated and constipated. That his stomach hurts and he's nauseas. I can tell you with absolute certainly that when he complains about being gassy, it's all too true. Wugh! Stand clear!"

Robert's father held his nose and waved his other hand around, clearing the fog.

Robert wanted to know if he'd seen a doctor.

"The doctor says he must stay away from foods made of wheat, barley and rye. It was easy to keep him from eating bread—I let him eat cake! But his Scotch whiskey was a problem, since it's made from the three forbidden grains. However, I was able to solve the dilemma. I weened him from Scotch by teaching him the delights of champagne. Now we drink wonderful champagne and dance together in the living room all evening (although, sometimes it sounds as if we are being pushed along by a little put-put motor)."

Robert had no doubt that Franzi was totally dedicated to his father. The empty kilo tins of caviar, the jars that once held the best Urbani truffles and the massive pile of dead soldier Goût de Diamant champagne bottles, with their expertly hand cut Swarovski crystal emblems, all lay gorgeously abandoned.

As his father didn't seem to be dying right then, Robert returned to school.

After some weeks or months, Robert returned to find Franzi sitting on the front porch. "Your father passed away some time ago."

She told him how it happened. "It was a progressive disease. He couldn't move around by himself so I brought him his food in bed and cleaned his soiled sheets. Of course, we enjoyed each other's company. Finally, on that last night, he couldn't hold down his champagne. He kept vomiting caviar. But he was merry and he demanded more. We sang a bit and drank our champagne. He vomited. I cleaned it up. We sang some more. And so the night passed. When I woke in the morning, he was by my side, quiet, and I knew he was gone," she said. "I did my best for him. But now I am a widow again."

Robert said to console her, "You really are a saint. A female St. Francis."

"Franzi is short for 'Franziska', which means 'little fisherwoman.'" she said. "Even though the name comes from Italian. My parents really named me for Giovanni Bernardone, who became Saint Francis of Assisi."

"Isn't he the one with all the animals and the birds on his shoulders?"

"Yes. I love the little birds." she said, without irony.

"But you don't believe you're a saint?"

"Well, some people think I might be. But not St. Francis. More of a modern saint, maybe. That nun from India. I like what she said: 'Of course, all my patients die. But they die with a smile on their faces.' Let that be my hallmark."

6. Who Is Sylvia?

AFTER HIGH SCHOOL, Robert hung around with some of the locals from wealthy families. "They were the bad, rich kids whose parents every so often kicked them out of their big homes. The parents had lots of money, but the kids were broke. So, they lived under the highway bridge near the golf club."

"These were rich kids living under a highway? They didn't have any money? How did they eat?"

"Well, most of their families were members of the club. They'd go over to the club restaurant and put things on their parents' tab. Their parents would pay the bills."

I'd never heard of anything like this. I wasn't sure I could believe him. "What did they do in the winter when it was freezing? They couldn't live under a bridge and freeze to death."

"Oh, they had a strategy," Robert said. "Every winter, when their parents flew down to some place warm, the kids would follow."

"So, all was forgiven? They'd live with their parents?"

"Oh no. If their parents wouldn't take them back, they had another strategy. They'd find another highway bridge and live under that."

Unlike his friends, who he said, were trapped in their dependencies on the family wealth, Robert felt free enough from that ilk—and poor enough—to find work driving a taxi.

"I thought you didn't drive," I said.

He waved that away. "Let me tell you what happened."

Robert's first fare one night was a woman with luggage who had just stepped off the train. When they reached her home on Moses Lane, Southampton, she asked Robert to help her carry her bags. The front door opened into the living room, and Robert came to an abrupt halt at the fireplace. "There was the painting, dominating the room" he said. "It was a standard kind of family portrait in almost every way.

93

Nicely lit. Everyone dressed in formal clothes. I could recognize the woman I'd just driven, but as a younger person. Next to her was a kid with a cocky look. Must have been her brother. There was an older lady who must be the mother, and she's standing next to someone I assume was the father. And that was the shock," Robert said. "The man was dressed in a full clown costume! White face, big red nose and the floppy shoes. It really got me."

"Cognitive dissonance," I said.

"Was it a joke? The woman saw me staring at it, but she didn't say anything. She paid the cab fare and handed me a tip. But then she caught my eyes and her stare froze me. Was she imitating the way I'd been staring at her painting? Mocking me? Making a private joke out of it?"

"Then what did she do?"

"She smiled. A nice smile. Friendly. And then I left."

As if something had been arranged behind his back, for the following five Fridays, Robert met the woman at the train. The first Friday, his cab was at the head of the taxi line and the dispatcher sent her to him. The second week, the same thing happened. From then on, Robert made sure to position himself first in line to meet her train. By that time they'd begun to talk and become friendly.

Her name was Sylvia. Over a cup of tea in her living room, Sylvia explained the mysterious painting. "My family is European. We have always been in show business, in the circus. My parents were famous, especially my father. In Europe they have more respect for clowns, more understanding of what they mean to the culture, than Americans have."

They came to this country when Sylvia was twelve. They'd been hired to appear on the Ed Sullivan TV program. They performed a sensational stunt: the whole family, dressed as clowns, fit inside an upright piano on the stage, and her father reached through an opening and played "The Stars and Stripes Forever" on the keys. "He played it backwards, you know?"

"The music? Backwards?" said Robert.

"Not the music, silly," Sylvia said. "Daddy was inside the piano, not in front of it. Backwards. You see?"

In the circus, Sylvia wore colorful silk costumes. "Of course, I performed acrobatics, juggling and some character acts. I even paraded around the ring on stilts. But my specialty was *corde lisse*, the aerial rope. I climbed as high as the top of the arena and then, while hanging upside-down, I waved my arms, gesturing hypnotically."

Robert told me that this was a lot of novel information to take in. At one point he got around to asking her: "But what do you mean, you gestured hypnotically?"

Her answer was mysterious. "Oh, that is what we do in the circus. Gesture hypnotically. It is the misdirection. The illusion that makes the circus magic." She then lifted her arms and waved them about gracefully for a moment. She smiled. "That is my gesture for you."

"But you're not still in the circus, right? What do you do now?"

"I act, when I can get the work. Otherwise, I have a business in the city."

Sylvia told him about a recent acting job. "It was Disney World. A big part they promised. I had to diet for a month to get back to performing weight. I ate nothing but Kiwi fruit. I lost twenty pounds. They flew me to Orlando. They measured me for my costume. It turned out, I was to be Minnie Mouse! A big padded suit with a Papier-mâché helmet. All that dieting for nothing! I could have weighed four hundred pounds and the damn costume would have fit!"

Robert had told Sylvia a little about himself. When he described his family's home on Gardiner's Bay, she seemed interested and asked him to show it to her. That Friday, when he picked her up at the train station, she said: "Let's drive out to see your house. I'll pay the fare."

They parked down the road and walked the rest of the way. When they turned the corner and reached the house, Robert pointed to it.

"Very dramatic," said Sylvia. "The way you suddenly made it appear. That's what I mean: You gestured hypnotically. I'm entranced."

Robert tried to see the family home through Sylvia's eyes. He saw the drama of it, the porticos for horses, the Widow's Walk up above the third floor.

After that visit, Robert said Sylvia began to treat him differently. She paid more attention when Robert shared with her his complex and thoroughly tangled ideas about the nature of existence. She began to ask him questions about his family and his house. How long had they lived there? How many rooms in the house? Did they have servants? And even, what would be the value of the place if it were put on the market?

In answer to Robert's earlier question, Sylvia told him that she managed a business in the city. A small business that she could run even if she were hired to be in a play.

"What kind of business?" said Robert.

Sylvia seemed reluctant to answer, but finally said, "We provide a service. When visiting businessmen come to the city for a big event requiring them to have an escort, they don't know any women to accompany them. So, we provide escorts. Our escorts are all beautiful and dress impeccably. They all speak two or three foreign languages. Because of this we're able to attract an international clientele. All very respectable, of course. Very high class."

Robert thought it sounded respectable, classy and certainly very sophisticated.

"Perhaps someday you'll visit me in the city. I'd like to show you around."

A visit to the city sounded dangerous to Robert. People who live closer to the city, or those who live elsewhere might find it hard to believe that there are people on Eastern Long Island who are born and die without once having toured the city, just 80 miles away. Although he had passed through the city underground on the railroad on the way to one or another of his prep schools, Robert was one of those.

When Robert admitted this Sylvia was aghast. "You mean you live within one hundred miles of the greatest city in the world and you've never seen it?"

Sylvia made it her mission to drag Robert to the city by any means. She put together an itinerary for seeing the Manhattan sites. "You can stay in my apartment. I have several roommates, but they won't bother us."

A few days before Robert was to meet Sylvia in Penn Station, he was watching the news on television. "I'm watching the end of a story about purse snatching and suddenly, you won't believe this, the story switches to Sylvia. She's right there on camera, and she's surrounded by cops. It's a raid on her business. She's acting brave. She keeps saying, 'This is a legitimate escort service!' Can you believe this? 'This is a legitimate escort service!' She's under arrest!"

I asked if we could help, though I couldn't see how.

"She's okay. She called me afterwards. She said it was all a mistake. It would be straightened out soon. And our city adventure was still on."

Sylvia met Robert at Penn Station. They took a cab uptown to a restaurant and then another, downtown to Sylvia's apartment. Throughout, Sylvia seemed, understandably, distracted.

Robert thought it would be tactful to refrain from asking her about the recent police trouble, but while they were eating she volunteered some information. "It's a legitimate escort service. Our clients pay in advance and I select the girl I think is appropriate for the event. Now, if a girl wants to offer the gentleman something else after she's fulfilled her responsibility to me, then that's her affair."

97

"Then what was all the trouble with the police?" Robert said.

Sylvia shrugged. "Apparently some of the girls got together at a bachelor party which got too raucous. The police came and found literature from my escort service. The girls all said they worked for me. The sergeant who came to arrest me addressed me as "Madam." I am not a madam!"

At Sylvia's apartment, she introduced Robert to her roommates. There seemed to be about eight of them, each with a little room only wide enough for a bed. "Normally, they're a happy crew, and we get along well. But some of these girls were ticketed in that raid. So, they're understandably a bit angry."

Two of the girls were immediately interested in Robert. "Oh, I like this one," the first girl said to Sylvia. "Yeah," said the other girl, "I might want some of that, too."

Robert told me he was a little taken aback. Sylvia said to pay no attention. The girls had been drinking red jug wine and offered Robert a glass, but Sylvia pulled him away. "Come into my room. I've got a special bottle I've been saving for us."

And, indeed, it was a special bottle: a Château Margaux. Robert recognized it from his father's cellar. "One of our clients gave it to me as a thank you for keeping his secrets," she said. "I'm very good at keeping secrets," she said. "Or … not."

They drank the delicious wine, its effect almost hallucinogenic. At some point Robert was alone in the room. Then he heard Sylvia calling him from the bathroom. He opened the door and found Sylvia naked in the bubble bath. "Come join me," she said, moving her arms in hypnotic gesture. Before he knew it, Robert was naked too, and sitting in the bubbles with her.

Sylvia began to soap Robert's chest. "Oh," she said, looking down. "I see you've brought a submarine. I can see its periscope rising."

"I'm not quite sure what went on after that. At one point I looked up and there were at least five naked women in the bathroom and I think they were all gesturing hypnotically."

"What happened?"

"Don't mess around with angry hookers," Robert said.

"But what did they do?"

He shook his head and smiled shyly. "They savaged me," he said. "Savaged me. Again and again."

7. Massive Diner Food

AFTER THAT, ROBERT'S taxi career was brief. His cab-driving territory was demarcated by the Hampton's two Greek diners: the one on Montauk Highway just west of Hampton Bays, and the one at the intersection of Montauk Highway and North Highway, at the eastern end of Southampton.

At first, Robert had been happy driving. "Wes, my dispatcher, gave me great advice. He said, 'You gotta know the streets'. I said, 'Wes, there's such wisdom in that! You gotta know the streets. Don't you think that's a great rule for life?'

"Wes tossed a map to me. 'I don't know what the hell you're talking about. You don't know this goddamn map by Tuesday, I'm going to fire your ass.'"

Despite Wes' warning, it had taken Robert a long time to learn how to negotiate even the main streets. So Wes limited him to pickups in the vicinity of one diner and drop-offs in the vicinity of the other, more or less on a safe, straight line that connected both.

After a couple of months, his break-time snacking got him well-known at both diners. He'd take his morning break at the Southampton diner and his late afternoon break at the diner in Hampton Bays. Both diners made enormous baked goods, such as cakes, crullers, and bear claws, and exotic Greek treats, such as olive bread, elassona, kaseri, rice pudding with thyme honey, marmalades, farsala halvas, milk pie and something called frumenty. Robert, with the gustatory energy of his glutton father, tried all of these. In three months, he'd gained thirty pounds.

"And then," Robert said. "The trouble started."

At the Southampton diner, the counterman always greeted him with, "What do ya want, *malaka?*"

Robert assumed '*malaka*' meant "kid," or "buddy" or some such informality. But on one occasion, when he came in later than usual, the counterman asked him what had happened. "I overslept," Robert said.

"Ah," said the counterman. "Too much *malakia*, I think!"

The other countermen laughed loudly. One of them, in passing, leered at Robert and slapped his back.

Robert found this bewildering. So, on his next visit to the Hampton Bays diner he called over a counterman who wasn't busy and said, "When I'm at the other diner, they call me '*malaka*'. Does that mean 'kid' or something? Or what does it mean?"

The counterman moved his eyes away from Robert. "No, no," he said. "I cannot tell you that. It is not nice."

"Come on," said Robert. "Tell me what it means. They're always calling me that."

"Well," the counterman said with a smirk, which he turned away from Robert quickly. "I tell you a secret. '*Malaka*' means you a jerk-off."

"And," said Robert apprehensively. "When they tell me 'too much *malakia*' it means….?"

"Yeah. It means you jerk-off too much, maybe."

Flabbergasted, Robert asked the man, "Well, tell me something I can say back to him after he calls me '*malaka*.'"

"I donno. Maybe call him '*poostie*.'"

"What does '*poostie*' mean?"

"It mean you an 'ass-fucker.'"

Armed with this weapon, Robert returned to the Southampton diner.

"It went like clock-work," said Robert. "No sooner did I walk in when the counterman shouted, 'Hey *Malaka*. What d'you want today?' And I shot back, 'Give me a cup of coffee, *Poostie*!'"

Hearing this, all the countermen stopped what they were doing, stunned. Then they began to laugh at the counterman who had greeted me, pointing and shouting in Greek.

Now, Robert believed, he'd gained some respect. The counterman stopped taunting him with '*malaka*'.

Life continued normally for a month or so. But one afternoon when Robert sat down for a pastry at the Hampton Bays diner, a new counterman came up to him and said, "What d'you want, *Malaka?*"

"I answered him automatically, "Robert said. "I couldn't help myself."

Robert had blurted out: "Give me a bear claw, *Poostie.*"

Unlike his experience at the Southampton diner, there was no other countermen around to laugh. And, in fact, this counterman wasn't laughing. Glowering, the man picked up a long kitchen knife and approached Robert. In a menacing whisper he said, "Now I gonna have to kill you!"

Terrified, Robert turned and ran from the diner. "I will never go back to that place," he told me.

Still, his decision to abandon the Hampton Bays diner limited his options for an afternoon snack. If he stuck to his route, he would have to wait until he returned to Southampton in order to get something.

"I suppose it was inevitable," he told me. "Sooner or later I knew it would happen. I walked into the Southampton diner one morning, and there was the counterman from Hampton Bays. I watched him pick up a knife and look daggers at me. I got the hell out of there. That day I quit driving the cab."

"There were plenty of other routes you could have driven that didn't involve going into the dangerous diners."

"Yeah," said Robert. "But I guess I screwed up. I don't know why. When it came down to it, I really didn't know the streets. I was only pretending that I did."

8. Wanda

"DID YOU KNOW," Robert said, "that I was once married?"

He said the marriage, now defunct, continued to be a mystery to him.

"Maybe a week or so after we got married, we were in Southampton. Wanda—that was my wife—went off somewhere to shop, and I was in Keene's bookstore, just browsing.

"Time passed, and I began to wonder where Wanda had got to. Had she gotten lost? Southampton was not a big village—only a few connected streets—with shops and banks, etcetera.

"More time passed, and I began to speculate: I wondered if, since our marriage, instead of learning to better recognize each other from among the faceless people in the street, we had forgotten what each other looked like."

Worse, he feared that when Wanda finally returned he would not be able to identify her.

"I blamed my confusion on our engagement and on everything that followed."

Robert didn't know how it happened. So far as he was concerned, they enjoyed a mild pleasure in each other's company—and that, not every day. They had been drifting without destination through the town one weekend afternoon when she tugged at his arm, interrupting his dream.

"Let's go into that jewelry store. They've got something there I want you to see."

He followed her into the store, and his eye was immediately drawn to the fine watch counter. "Don't dawdle," she scolded. She led him to the cabinet that displayed diamond engagement rings, objects that had never interested him, since he knew he would never wear one. She pointed to a large diamond mounted on a filigreed band. "Isn't that gorgeous? Don't we just love it?"

"It's quite lovely," Robert said, trying to sound interested.

"I fell in love with it as soon as I saw it a few weeks ago." And then in a playful voice, "Were you thinking the same thing I was thinking?"

That was a hard one. "What were we thinking?"

"Oh, just that, you know, if we ever thought about getting married, this would be the ring you would buy for me."

"Certainly," he assured her with as much confidence as he could muster. "That would surely be the ring, if we were thinking about, you know, that… er, doing that."

She seemed genuinely happy, and he did not discourage her when she asked the saleswoman if she could try it on. To his surprise, the ring fit her finger perfectly, as if it had been made for her. "You see," she said modeling the ring before his eyes. "Doesn't it look pretty?"

Again, he felt called upon to reassure her, and happily agreed that it looked superbly pretty.

She motioned him aside, out of the saleswoman's hearing. "You know, darling," she began, and he quaked at the word 'darling'. "You know, a ring as pretty as that might be sold right away. Maybe, you know, just in case we ever decided we wanted to get married, maybe we should put a deposit on it, just so they'll hold it for us?"

Cautiously, he told her that that seemed the logical precaution to take, in the circumstances. But he found himself gasping for air, desperate to buy time.

"Good," she told him. "I'd hoped you'd say that." She turned to the saleswoman who had been standing behind the counter waiting for Wanda, though there were other customers in the store needing attention. "Can we put a deposit on that ring?" she asked.

The saleswoman said yes, but only if we were planning to pay the balance within a few days. "Oh," Wanda said disappointed, and turned to him. "That's too bad."

He agreed that it was too bad, and contrived to put on a sad face.

"There is something else you can do," the saleswoman said after a moment.

"Yes?" Wanda asked, and Robert put on a happy face.

"If you took the layaway option, you could leave a deposit on the ring now and take up to two years to pay it off. Would you be interested in that?"

Robert saw a chance to play the gallant and immediately agreed that that was a good idea. After all, much can change in two years. It was a good way to buy time.

And Wanda seemed pleased. With her encouragement, he allowed the saleswoman to charge a deposit to his new credit card, with similar increments to be deducted monthly. He could always get the purchase price back, she assured him, if, for some reason, they decided not to take the ring. Wanda and Robert made reassuring sounds to the clerk, and then left the store.

"You know," Wanda told him over the French fries. "I've just been calculating the interest on that ring. It's going to be a lot, almost enough to buy two rings when we're finished paying for it."

She showed him the computations she'd been making on the back of the lunch receipt and he had to agree with her: the interest was indeed excessive, almost, usurious. "Too bad we don't have enough money to buy the ring right now," she lamented.

Her lament rubbed against his pride. Yes, it was indeed a great deal of interest to pay! So why not buy the ring now and keep it until—or if—they decided to go through with the engagement? He'd save a lot of money, and he'd hide the ring in some safe cache until the event. "You know," he told her. "I think you're right. Why don't we do this: why don't we buy the ring right now and put it away until we decide what we're going to do?"

Wanda appeared to think. "Yes," she adjudicated. "It's a lot of money to lay out for something we don't know will ever happen, but it is the right thing to do, financially. You're a good businessman, my dearest. Let's do it!"

So, they bought the ring. Instead of hiding it away, Wanda asked if she could wear it for a bit, at least until he drove her to her parent's home on Dune Road. The ring did look wonderful on her finger, and as they drove the twenty minutes to her house, they fantasized on what married life would be like.

It was an enjoyable trip. To their surprise, when they pulled up to the curb in front of her house, Wanda's family was standing there waiting. Wanda opened the door and held up her left hand to show her parents. "Look what we've bought!"

"You're engaged!" her family proclaimed in joyous unison.

And so they were, from that moment on.

What followed was, for Robert, a blur lasting several months. Wanda's mother, sisters, aunts and other female relations took over their lives. Happily for Robert—or, less unhappily—he was left out of most campaigns. He discovered early on that this was to be all about Wanda.

The most vexing thing, aside from the marriage ceremony and reception (during which Wanda force-fed him with sticky, sugary, wedding cake), was the seeming necessity that Wanda and he play these curious roles: first, the Engaged Couple, and then the Married Couple. The misdirection inherent in this role-playing, Robert believed, was the behavior that caused him to fear, as he stood there awkwardly in Keene's bookstore, that he would not recognize Wanda when she eventually found her way back.

Robert remained abstracted, rooted to the spot, for an hour. When he came to and focused his eyes, he was gazing into those of a woman. "You look lost," said the woman. "Have I kept you waiting long?"

It was Wanda, or, at least, she seemed to be Wanda. "Are you all right?" He ached for some familiar cue to identify her.

"Yes," she answered. "Yes," I think I'm all right. It's just that I got lost looking for some gift to surprise you …." She hesitated, then asked, "You are my husband, aren't you?"

"Yes, yes of course I am. And you are my wife?"

"Oh," she answered, initiating the first and last truly intimate moment they were to have. "Forgive me. It's only that I've been in such a haze since the wedding."

Robert thought it was his role to reassure her. "It's all right," he said. "You and I are going to be all right."

They left the store together, arm in arm. Yet, as they walked into the sunshine to his parked car he asked himself if this woman he was with was, indeed, the real Wanda? Was it possible this woman, this stranger had misplaced her own newly wedded husband and come upon him in error? That he was a confused husband who had misplaced his newly wedded wife and, against all odds, accepted some substitute?

He asked himself these questions with mounting suspicion. And after several years, he told me, he's now come to believe the most radical answer. They, in fact, were not the same people who first met, taking mild pleasure in each other's company. Like the unfortunate children who wake from panicked dreams desperate to know if they'd been mistakenly placed with the wrong parents, Wanda and Robert had also been victimized, a hapless couple switched at the altar by forces beyond understanding.

"And what's more is," he said. "I don't know, but I suspect there are many others like us."

9. She Walks Out

ON THEIR WEDDING night, comfortable in bed in a New York City hotel overlooking Central Park, Wanda said: "I need to tell you that you are not the only man I plan to sleep with. I believe in honesty. I hope you understand."

Robert thought about it. Yes, honesty was very important in a relationship. It was comforting to know that he had an honest wife.

"And," Wanda said. "I hope you don't mind if we don't have children. I hate the idea of children. Don't you detest them?"

Robert considered this. He'd never thought about having children. He liked them well enough. But his own? That seemed a decision for the far away future, perhaps for another lifetime.

He'd done his duty, he reflected. He'd gone through with Wanda's and her family's plans. He'd demonstrated civility and restraint during the interminable engagement. After the grueling ceremony and reception at Wanda's Dune Road home, Robert thought, "Well, that's that," and just assumed that this had all been for show and he was ready to resume his bachelor's life. It came as a shock to him that Wanda was still to be in the picture. "We're going to New York City for our honeymoon," she said. "Have you forgotten?"

Robert wanted to tell her to go on without him. He'd look forward to saying hello to her when she returned. But he was tired now, and needed a nap. However, something told him that that might not be an appropriate response. It was the truth, of course. And Wanda appreciated the truth. But, no. He wouldn't say it.

When they returned from their honeymoon, Robert discovered that he had neglected to make a critical down payment on the house Wanda had chosen for them in Southampton, near Wanda's parents. The house had already been sold. Wanda, outraged, hectored Robert relentlessly to find another home for them. "And," Robert recalled

Wanda warning him. "It had better be all I've been dreaming of. Everything my family expects!"

After rushing from broker to broker, Robert found a place that both of them could accept. The house in Watermill had once been a potato barn (which appealed to Robert) but had been converted by its previous owner, an occasionally successful landscape painter, into a showplace with hot tubs, large living rooms and dining rooms and a fifteen-foot high stone fireplace above which hung a fifteen foot-high cut glass chandelier (all of which appealed to Wanda). The artist had been forced to sell in order to pay legal fees resulting from several cases of child pornography for which he'd been indicted. Wanda concluded that they'd gotten a bargain worth perhaps twice as much as they'd paid for it.

Wanda had insisted on having at least two servants. Robert agreed but stood his ground when it came to engaging a butler. "I was more or less a free-spirited hippie then," Robert said. "What kind of hippie has a butler?"

Wanda declared that Robert, who had long ago quit his taxi driving job, find daytime work. She didn't want him hanging around the house. "Why don't you let my father set you up in one of the family businesses? Why don't you go into town and get yourself some respectable clothes? Start to dress like someone I would want to go to a country club dance with."

But Robert resisted. He couldn't see himself sitting at a desk somewhere. Having to join one of his father-in-law's New York City clubs. He thought that if he simply followed Wanda's directions he'd end up in a trap from which he'd never escape.

Thus, Robert hit the road looking for work.

"I didn't know where to begin," Robert said. "One day I was driving somewhere, taking a shortcut on Snake Hollow Road in Bridgehampton to avoid the tourist traffic. I was passing the grounds where they hold the Hampton Classic Horse Show every year. My family never owned horses, but I'd taken riding lessons when I was eight or nine. I thought maybe I could work for them, be a jockey."

"That's ridiculous," I said. "First of all, you're way too tall. You know how short real jockeys are?"

"Well, I thought I'd try, anyway. I drove down to Riverhead, where they keep horses for the Horse Show, and I asked for a job. I told the old guy who was there about my expertise as a rider, and that I was considering this for a career.

"The old guy said they didn't have jobs for jockeys, but I could start by getting 'up close and personal' with horses. I asked him what was involved, and he said, 'You gotta shovel a little horseshit.'

"I thought, Ah ha. Here was another great maxim, like 'You gotta know the streets'. I mean," Robert said. "Doesn't it say so much about life? When you start out, you always have to shovel a little horseshit."

"So, what was the job like?"

"I admit I was surprised. I showed up at four in the morning. The old guy handed me a pitchfork and pointed to the stables. He said, 'Get in there and shovel out all the horseshit.' I was shocked! I hadn't taken him literally."

"What did you do?"

"I did as he said: I got in there with a bunch of other guys with pitchforks and we all shoveled."

Around ten in the morning, Robert's third day, a group of children from a local school arrived to ride the horses around the bridal path.

"I was out behind the stables with a bunch of the guys. We were drinking whiskey from a bottle in a paper bag. The old guy came over and told me that the kids needed someone to lead them around the bridal path. 'You told me you were a rider,' the old guy said. 'Show me what you can do. Lead those kids around the track and bring 'um back to the stables. Remember, though: Don't let your horse do more than a trot. Those kids are just learning.'"

Robert continued. "So, one of the guys picked out a horse for me. 'She's a good one,' he told me with a wink. 'Very calm and gentle.' He even saddled her for me. I got on and rode over to head up the line of kids on their horses." Robert paused for a moment, recalling the scene. "We started out, just walking along the path through the woods. All of a sudden, without any warning, my horse took off. Before I knew it, we were galloping. I'd never galloped before. I pulled on the reins to get her to slow down, but she just kept running faster. All I could do was hold onto the saddle horn. Every once in a while, the horse would take me under a low tree branch, and I'd have to duck. She did this so often, I really believed she was trying to knock me off!"

"What happened?" I asked.

"We just kept galloping. The kids were way behind me, out of sight. I kept holding on for dear life until the horse ran around the path and reached the stables, where she stopped, throwing me over the side. I was shaken, as you can imagine.

"The old guy scurried over and grabbed the reins. 'What the hell are you trying to do? I didn't hire you to be a cowboy and scare hell out of those kids. Get off the ground and get off this property!'

"Well, I didn't know what to say. I walked back past the guys leaning against the stable, still taking shots from the whisky bottle. I could see them grinning, trying not to show it. The guy who'd picked out the horse for me said, 'I guess I should have given you a slower horse. Maybe one with three legs.' Then they all laughed.

"That was it for me with that job," Robert said.

That night Robert returned to the house and found it empty. There was no one home and the furniture, carpets, and pictures were gone. Had they been robbed? Had Wanda been kidnapped? But there was no ransom note.

Robert stayed alone for two nights, sleeping on a pile of clothes on the floor, waiting to hear from Wanda or from somebody. Finally, he packed whatever he could find and left the house for good. "I said, to hell with her family's money. If Wanda could walk away from our marriage, so could I. And I've never heard a word from her since."

Robert was silent for several minutes, pensive. Then he asked: "Do you have a little voice in your head that gives you advice? I mean, everybody talks about getting advice from a little voice in their heads."

I told him yes, I sometimes heard a voice in my head. I called it the Voice of Common Sense.

"Oh," said Robert. "I've wondered about that. The Voice of Common Sense. I wonder what that's about?"

10. Manners

WE WERE EATING breakfast in Speed's when I felt I had to interrupt Robert as he was stuffing food into his mouth with both hands. "Listen to me," I said. "You can't carry on like this in a public restaurant."

"What do you mean?"

"I mean it's bad enough when we're at home. I enjoy your enthusiasm at the dinner table. But you've got to use some manners in public."

"Manners. What do you mean, 'manners'?"

"I mean you've got to use your knife, fork and spoon. When you have soup, you use a soup spoon. You don't lift the bowl and drink from it. When you eat meat, you don't stab it with your fork and shove it in your mouth. You spend a little time with it. You cut it into mouth-sized bites. And, what's really important," I said, "is that you stop snorting and gurgling while you're doing it."

"I don't know what you mean."

"Watch the way I eat. Look at the other people eating right around us. We're all using the cutlery. It's politeness, it's civility."

"I guess I forgot all that at boarding school. Everybody there ate the way I did, especially when they served us spaghetti and lasagna. Then you'd see enthusiasm! First, the head of the table would take the bowl of pasta that was meant for all seven of us, and dump it on his plate. Then he'd tell the waiter to bring us more. The next bowl went to the guy sitting to his right. The next to the guy on his left. And so on, down the table. Screw the knives and forks. We gulped the stuff down and demanded thirds and fourths!"

"Yes. Well. We're not in boarding school here."

"Okay. I'll try to follow your example."

I wasn't surprised by Robert's ignorance of basic etiquettes and conventions. There were many other situations where I thought he needed advice. For instance, when someone did him a favor, I had to explain how the polite thing to do would be to offer to do something for that person in return. He didn't understand the concept of tipping. "You give the server a tip for decent service" I said. "But if your server gives you great service, you give the server something extra." Eating together at a restaurant, I showed him how to calculate the tip. I sternly lectured him on the correct way of asking a table mate to pass some item: "You don't yell, 'Pass the fucking butter!'" I told him. I also had to remind him that when we got up to leave, it was not polite to throw one's napkin on the floor.

I should have anticipated that the effect of this frequent instruction would be that Robert would begin to rely on me, even to cling.

He told me that I was his best friend. "I think you're the only one who can get me out of this place!"

I had no idea what he was talking about.

"I don't mean this *place*," he said. "Not my house. Not the college. I mean my—what?—my destiny."

"What destiny?"

"I don't want to be one of those privileged guys I grew up with at boarding school. One of these exiles, living under bridges in fashionable parts of the world. One way or another, they're all dependent on their families. My mother's always inviting me back home. It would be so easy to fall into that easy life." He looked at me with great sincerity and whispered: "You're the only one who can help me. I want to be just like you. I want to be happy making my own way in the world!"

What he said felt cloying and creepy. Maybe he was getting too close for my comfort. "I'm not your best friend," I told him harshly, and I could see I'd wounded him.

One morning Robert hitchhiked to the college. I'd had a late night and was only now getting up and dressed. I was annoyed when I couldn't find any clean underwear. I was frustrated that one of my new shirts had disappeared, as well as my sports coat.

114

When I arrived on campus, I ran into another student whom I knew slightly. He stood there, looking at me with curiosity.

"Do you have a twin going to school here?" he asked.

"No," I said. "Why?"

"And you can't be in two places at once, correct?"

"Right," I said.

"Then who is that over there in the cafeteria who dresses exactly like you?"

And, of course, it was Robert, wearing my sports coat, jeans and boots. They were so tight on him, it reminded me of the Lewis Carrol illustrations for Twiddle Dumb and Twiddle Dee. When I got closer to him, I saw he had combed his hair in my style.

"What's going on here?" I asked, pointing at my clothes he was wearing.

"It's laundry day," he said, nervously. "My clothes are at the cleaners. I didn't think you'd mind if I borrowed yours."

"My underwear, too?"

"Well, I ran out of my own."

"Listen, Robert," I said with finality. "I know that imitation is flattery. But you've gone too far. Let's keep it this way: You wear your own clothes and I'll wear mine. You make the best of being yourself and I'll be myself. You're not me. Don't try to be me. It won't work."

11. Robert on the Rebound

AFTER WANDA'S DESERTION, Robert told me he'd hung around the Hansom House, a bar in Southampton next to the train station. He drank a bit too much each night, but he met lots of girls, mostly from the college.

One morning while he was in bed nursing a terrible hangover, his telephone woke him up. A girl was calling all excited. "I'm so happy!" she said. "To think that you and I are going to be married!"

"I had no idea who she was or how I'd gotten into this situation. But one thing I knew: There was something really familiar about this situation. Familiar and scary. So I hung up the phone and never answered it again.

Another time, Robert met a woman at a party in Amagansett. She was celebrating her divorce. She kept shouting, "Come on! Let's everyone be happy!"

"It was late," Robert told me. "I admit I was drunk. I wanted to go home, but she insisted we go dancing. 'I'm too tired', I pleaded."

"What are you? Sixty? Seventy? A hundred?" she taunted. "Is it baby's bedtime?"

"Alright," he said. "Let's go."

Several of them got into a big car parked out back. She climbed onto the hood. "Who do you think you are? Zelda Fitzgerald?" someone called out.

They arrived at the bar, Stephen Talkhouse, and she slid off. "I might have to be sick a little later on," she confided.

"I had to borrow money to get us in the door," Robert said. "We danced and drank. She offered to let me stay with her for the night."

"I've got some Champagne and a canopy bed," she declared.

Her house was a dark outline on the beach. "We have to be awfully quiet," she told Robert. "We can't wake my daughter."

They stumbled through her living room without lights, feeling their way with toes and fingers. She flicked the switch. Her bedroom was brilliant: damask curtains, an Aubusson carpet, and lacy material bridging the posts of her bed. They drank the Champagne and undressed with the lights on. Her bed was like an operating theater. "I could see the veins in her breasts and thighs delineated as if on an x-ray."

They began to caress, but she pulled away. "Wait," she said. "What am I doing? I can't do this. It's too soon. You'll have to leave."

She gathered his pants and shoes and pushed him out of the room. "Be careful," she warned. "Don't wake my daughter." He crawled along the floor looking for the back door.

"God damn it, I'm lost!" he whispered, hoping she would hear.

Robert continued: "It seemed like an hour when later I found my way out. I drove home, Brahms blaring loud on the radio keeping me awake while I got lost in the woods between Amagansett and The Springs. I was furious. She made me believe I was the most attractive man at the party. And then what? Nothing?"

Robert had had a long time to rethink that night. He no longer hated her. It wasn't her fault. He had come to admire her courage to make a difficult decision, given the circumstances.

One evening he met her again at a Guild Hall opening. "You don't remember me," she said.

"Yes. Yes I do," Robert replied.

"I just wanted to tell you how sorry I was about what happened."

"Oh no," he said. "Don't worry about it."

"Well, thank you," she said. "But do you know something that's always bothered me?"

"What?" he asked.

"I was so wrapped up in my own troubles that I never asked you your name."

"'Ah', I said, nodding in understanding, smiling my most tolerant smile. 'That's okay,' I told her. 'It happens to us all.'

"What I didn't tell her," Robert added "Was that I had no idea what her name was, either."

12. The Voice of Common Sense

DURING THE SCHOOL year, Robert and I had entered our poems in a university writing contest. To our amazement, when the awards were given at the end of the semester, Robert had won First Prize. The prize came with a two-year fellowship at the University Center down the Island as a part-time English instructor and an editor of the university literary magazine.

"You see," I said when we got the news. "You've done it. You've got your start. This is the beginning of your real career. You won't be a lazy rich guy getting blotto every night. You'll be a writer and an editor—a professor! And even if you get drunk every night you won't be crying in your beer. You'll have something to celebrate, to be proud of."

Robert sighed. "It's a little frightening," he said.

The school year was almost over. I had been at the college collecting my last paycheck for house-sitting. I returned to the house in The Springs to pack my stuff. After spring vacation I would be moving back into the dorms. I'd taken an unpaid job as an editor of the campus newspaper, *The Windmill*. My mission was to assist the editor, a senior who had returned from the Vietnam War with some behavioral problems which I was supposed to mind.

Robert was home. "Franzie was here," he said. "You remember I told you about Franzie? My father's widow? She owns this house, you know. She's thinking of putting it on the market."

"Just at the right time, too," I said. "You'll be living down the Island. You won't have to worry about taking care of this place."

He seemed distracted. "You know, Franzie's planning on taking a cruise around the world for a year or two."

"Yes?" I said. "That's nice. How does that affect you?"

"She's invited me to go with her," he said.

During our time together, I'd developed an affection for Robert. I sensed danger and hurried to caution him about Franzie's invitation. "You're not thinking seriously about going with her?"

"Well, I had that thought."

"Why? You've won a big prize—a fellowship is worth something. How could you think of giving it up? I mean," I said, getting into it. "Aside from throwing away a great opportunity, you'd be putting yourself in the position of a kept man. Do you know what a kept man is?"

"Of course," Robert said. "Probably most of the men in my family have been kept. I suppose it wouldn't hurt to become one myself. A kind of tradition, right?."

"But think of this: Think of Franzie's history. She's like a black widow spider. All her mates have met their ends. That's what you told me."

"Oh, it would be different with me. I wouldn't be her mate."

"That's what you think. That's not what she's got planned. You'd be alone with her on board the ship, thousands of miles from home. She's paying your way. Don't you imagine that she'd expect something for that?"

"You mean that I'd die with a smile on my face, like all her husbands?"

"Exactly," I said. "Don't you dare even imagine it! Or, do imagine it and beware!"

"Hmm," he said. "A serious consideration. But do you remember when I asked you whether you'd ever heard a voice in your head that gave you advice? You called it the Voice of Common Sense."

"Yes," I said.

"Well, I finally heard that voice. Heard it loud and clear. I was sitting here on the couch, thinking about Franzie's trip. Should I go? Should I not? Then I heard the voice. It was as if someone, a real presence, had come in through my thoughts. It sat down next to me and it said, 'Haven't you been through enough? All these painful romances? Your marriage mysteriously evaporating? All the pieces of the puzzle still unconnected? Shouldn't you be spending your time connecting them?' Then the voice shouted something at me, shouted in the loudest human tone I'd ever imagined: 'You'd be a fucking idiot to go on that trip! A big fucking idiot!'"

Finally! I thought. I was happy for Robert. At last he'd found his Voice of Common Sense. "So, what did you tell Franzie?"

"Tell her?" he said and chuckled. "What do you think I told her? It was a luxury cruise around the world! How could anyone pass that up? 'Of course I'll go,' I told her. I mean, really. I'll get to the poetry later on. What have I got to lose?"

EPILOGUE

A Ghost Driving West

RIVING WEST ON Springs Fireplace Road on a winter morning in 1972, a shadow, a thought crossed my mind. The familiar scenery of woods, scant homes and the remnants of recent snowfall on the roadside seemed infused with meaning. Was this the last time I would see these things?

I was headed to Columbia University in the City of New York, where I would begin the Master of Fine Arts program. It didn't seem possible that I was deserting this place that had given me gifts of great value: friendships with the superb artists and writers from the region from whom I had learned the rudiments of my own craft. I had learned from their instruction, but I had learned even more by being a part of their lives: perceiving their quirks, flaws, failures and successes.

I wasn't looking for a sign that might endorse my journey, but I got one anyway.

I had to brake swiftly to avoid hitting a tall, thin man on a bicycle. I recognized him immediately as Willem de Kooning. Ironic, I thought. The last person I'd see as I left this place, would be the first person I saw when I'd moved out here.

Back then, on a summer evening, as I drove east towards my rental home on Gardiner's Bay, de Kooning's bicycle had swung out of a side road directly in front of my car. I had driven slowly behind him, watching him riding along, swerving figure eights from right to left, until he finally came to a stop. He was motionless on the bike for a moment, then pitched over gently into the uncut brush of the roadside.

"Hello," he said brightly when I'd helped him up. "Would you like a drink?"

"No thanks," I'd told him.

"Then would you please drive me home?"

I loaded the painter and his bicycle into my car. I followed his directions to the farmhouse where he lived, opposite the Green River Cemetery, a mile or so away. As I helped him out, he pointed and said, "All my friends are buried over there."

Now I was leaving, and it was as if he and I were reenacting our first meeting, but in reverse.

I pulled up alongside him.

"You!" he called out. "Watch where you're going. Do you want to hit me?"

He hadn't recognized me. The first time we'd met he'd been drunk. Now he seemed sober. Maybe drunkenness and sobriety were different worlds for him and I did not exist in this sober one.

In any case, I apologized, waved goodbye and passed on. Perhaps, I reflected, in de Kooning's eyes, as well as in my own, I was already gone from there, already become a ghost.

I drove on through Sagaponack, Bridgehampton, Watermill, Southampton and over the Shinnecock Canal, saying my sad farewells to each town. When I turned onto the westbound North Highway, my mood changed abruptly. I couldn't suppress sudden laughter.

I'd just realized that these farewells were phony and entirely unnecessary. This place, the East End of Long Island, was my New World, and, like Columbus, I would always return.

People, Places, Things and Acknowledgements

Introduction

For a fuller introduction to David Ignatow, H. R. Hays, Willem de Kooning, and others as I knew them in or around 1970, see my *A Hole In the Ocean: A Hamptons' Apprenticeship*, Marsh Hawk Press, 2016

H. R. Hays. *The Selected Poems of H.R. Hays, With Essays on Translation*, Edited by Sandy McIntosh, Xlibris Corp. 2000

David Ignatow. *Against the Evidence: Selected Poems, 1934–1994*, Wesleyan Poetry Series, 1994

Charles Matz. *Columbus, the Moor* Multilingual Edition, House of Nehesi, 2015

Ilya Bolotowsky. *Ilya Bolotowsky*. The Solomon R. Guggenheim Museum, 1974

Judith Zilcze. *Willem de Kooning: A Way of Living*. Phaidon Press, 2017

I

"Taking Reality Through Its Paces: Filmmaking With Norman Mailer and Ilya Bolotowsky." *Confrontation* No. 80/81, Fall 2002/Winter 2003

For events in the making of *Maidstone* that I didn't participate in, I rely on the accounts of Sally Beauman, J. Anthony Lucas and James Toback, which are reprinted in: *Maidstone, a Mystery*, by Norman Mailer. New York: Signet—New American Library, 1971

II

Jackson Pollock & Family. *American Letters, 1927–1947*. Polity Press, 2009

Sandy McIntosh. "H.R. Hays: The Theater of Disappointment". Talisman magazine, talismanmag.net. Talisman House, 2016

Caleb T. Boyd, "H. R. Hays' Red Play *A Song about America*: A Musical History Lesson and CPUSA Appeal to the African American Community," *Eisler-Mitteilungen* no. 65 (April 2018): 9–16.

Guild Hall Museum. *Poets and Artists of the Region Collaborating.*... 1982

III

Allen Planz. *A Night For Rioting*. The Swallow Press. 1969

Osha Neumann. *Up Against the Wall Motherf**er: A Memoir of the '60s, with Notes for Next Time*. Seven Stories Press, 2008

"Meeting Capote at Keene's in Southampton." "Coffee With Jean Stafford in The Springs". *Galatea Resurrects*, April 2018

Marcel Proust, James Grieve, trans. *In the Shadow of Young Girls in Flower: In Search of Lost Time*, Vol. 2. Penguin, 2005

> The English translation of Proust that I had first struggled to read was made by C. K. Scott Moncrieff and titled *Remembrance of Things Past*. From what I had learned about the original French of Proust, Moncrieff had not only provided an English version but also a reordering and polishing of Proust's disorderly, quirky, but perhaps more beautiful novel. James Grieve's translations correct this, getting us closer to Proust's results, if not his unrealized intentions.
>
> Proust's "granddaughter" quotes the title of Volume 2 as *Of Flowers and Virgins*. Moncrieff translates it as *From a Budding Grove*. Grieve's translation of the title is above.

IV: Teen Angel

"Teen Angel" by Mark Dinning. (1960). Ask Alexa to play it for you.

A Note on the Teaching the Poets Attempted in the East End Public Schools

Allen Planz and I—as well as other poets on the East End, including David Ignatow, Graham Everett, Ron Overton, Susan Astor, and Claire White, all rode the poetry teaching circuit, encouraging kids as young a nursery schoolers to create poems. While a creative writing teacher in a high school or college classroom might use class time for silent writing, this usually can't be done successfully with young kids. They need immediate and constant engagement. For the kids ages six on up, who could already print or write cursive (that dying art), we used creative exercises, some of which had been developed by Phillip Lopate and the late Kenneth Koch, a Columbia professor and Hamptons resident. Koch's brilliant assignments, such as "Write a letter to your shoe," or "Write your life story, but make it all lies," or "Write down a dream you had at night, but write it as if it really happened when you were awake," are designed to push kids into a poetic frame of mind, from whence they can create visions that delight themselves and others.

For the poet-teachers in the classroom, things didn't always go so well. Often, classroom teachers would resent an outsider's shanghaiing of their class. Some would try in subtle or bold ways to reclaim their students' attention for themselves, such as rocking very loudly in their chair at the back of the room, humming, or correcting the poet each time he said "You know?" as a way to fill a blank spot in his conversation. Against this chafing, we poets eventually devised ways to avoid the sabotage or, in extreme situations, humiliate the teacher (if we never wanted to return to that classroom again).

Throughout my teaching, I kept a journal in which I pondered exactly what this PITS program was trying to accomplish, and what it actually accomplished.

Here is the last page of that journal:

> What is missing in a kid's creative experience is solitude. That factor is prerequisite to the mature artist's ability to create. Solitude is first a condition of essential loneliness, an original human paradox, common to all but impossible to share. For a writer, solitude is in the beginning only a working condition, just part of the job as the freezing air is to a car mechanic who must work

128

outdoors in winter. Gradually, solitude becomes a kind of place itself. The experienced writer goes there to spread out his tools, like a surgeon, to get ready for the operation. At the same time, solitude is portable and accessible anywhere. Years spent alone, or months, days or hours are not necessary for the experienced writer to re-enter solitude. It is enough only to remember it, and you are there. Perhaps solitude is a glorified word for concentration. But I think it is a particular kind of concentration, won only by lone-standing commitment to writing—and this is the thing kids lack.

I must have lived in solitude until about kindergarten, and then I began moving out of it, confronted as I was by the lives of other children. Children become confused between the world of others and their own at a fairly early stage, and they are led to ignore their precious solitude by the tabula rasa dogma of the schools. The tabula rasa idea exists in every school I've taught in, no matter how open each says it is in its educational methodology. If teachers have abandoned the notion that humans have an innate capacity for creativity-which is the opposite of tabula rasa—and if teachers themselves do not any longer know how or care to create, how can they lead their students to create? Impossible!

Poets often talk about "getting the kids at the right age." What does that mean? They answer, "Get them before all the creativity has been talked out of them." But if the creativity goes out, where does it go?

Some exercises that poets use in the classroom bring the kids back to solitude. But, I bet that the ocean of the rest of the world, which itself does not want to go in the direction of solitude, will soon suggest more important directions.

When I talk about kids' poems, I am talking at the same time about poems that teachers, PTA, and others call "delightful" and poems that are genuinely good. The two are usually different. Teachers are interested in educational issues. PTAs are interested in kids having special experiences. Other support groups, like BOCES, are interested in providing alternatives-exciting changes. The people in these groups are often literary enthusiasts only, who do not (and why should they?) have the personal background in writing from which to tell what is good and what is not in kids' poetry. Their jobs often depend on a basically static, formula-oriented educational system, which attempts to contain the kids, much as a corral contains horses. Their training does not cover the possibility of the horses walking back and forth through the gates. Therefore when a kid does go outside the formulas, he or she is marked "absent," that is, invisible. I have found that when a poem written by a kid does make it outside the gates, I usually have to point out its virtues to the teacher. Some teachers do not understand me. I discovered this when working with a kindergarten class which I asked to draw pictures of different things that we would later relate to words and sounds. One assignment was to draw God. The kindergarten teacher nervously went around the room "correcting" the pictures by renaming any that she believed strayed from the "truth." For instance, one kid drew a snakelike monster and wrote beneath his drawing GOD. The teacher quickly crossed that out and wrote CREATURE.

Children have to be led to their solitude if they are to write poetry for real. Because of the nature of their educational environments, the probability of their finding solitude again before they have reached adolescence is small. For now, as one kid wrote yesterday when we were practicing similes, "Poetry is like nothing without the poet."

From "Poetry is Like Nothing Without the Poet," *Teachers & Writers Magazine*, Vol. 12, No. 2, Teachers & Writers Collaborative, 1981

About the Author

SANDY McINTOSH was born in Rockville Centre, New York, and received a BA from Southampton College, an MFA from Columbia University and a doctorate from the Union Graduate Institute and University. After working with children for eight years as a writer in the schools he completed a study of writers who taught in the program and how their work with children affected their own writing. The study, *The Poets in the Poets-in-the Schools* was published by the University of Minnesota. He alternated teaching creative writing at Southampton College and Hofstra University with publishing nonfiction works, such as *Firing Back* (John Wiley 1997), and computer software, such as *Mavis Beacon Teaches Typing!* (Electronic Arts, 1986). He contributes journalism, poetry, and opinion columns to *The New York Times*, *The Daily Beast*, *The New York Daily News*, *Newsday*, *The Nation*, *The Wall Street Journal*, *American Book Review*, and elsewhere. He was also editor and publisher of *Wok Talk*, a Chinese cooking bi-monthly and the author and editor of several Chinese cook books.

His first collection of poetry, *Earth Works*, was published by Southampton College in 1970, the year he graduated. He has since published 11 collections of poetry, four prose volumes and three computer software programs.

His original poetry in a screenplay won the Silver Medal in the Film Festival of the Americas. *The New York Times'* published his poem "Cemetery Chess," and an excerpt of his collaboration with Denise Duhamel appears in *The Best American Poetry*.

From 1990 to 2000 he was chairman of the Distinguished Poetry Series at Guild Hall, East Hampton, New York.

He was managing editor of Long Island University's national literary journal, *Confrontation*, for more than a decade, and is publisher of Marsh Hawk Press.

About the Cover Artist

KEN ROBBINS was a fine art photographer, commercial artist, and the writer/illustrator of more than twenty highly acclaimed children's books. He lived and made photographs in East Hampton, New York since 1972. He was born in Brooklyn, New York, in 1945, raised in West Orange, New Jersey, and graduated Cornell University in 1967 with a degree in English. After five years as a book editor in New York City, he moved to the East End of Long Island, and commenced a freelance career. He lived in The Springs with his wife, Maria.

Chapter One: On Becoming a Poet

The Chapter One Project from Marsh Hawk Press features the memoirs of outstanding poets from diverse backgrounds, recalling the ways by which they found their start as writers.

While creative writing programs seek to develop the talents of maturing writers, recondite but essential information about the development of the writing craft will be discovered in the early memoirs—the Chapter One's—of established poets published in this series.

For more information about Chapter One visit our Web site:
www.marshhawkpress.org